Venice &
the Veneto

Other books by James Bentley

Albert Schweitzer
Alsace
Bavaria
Between Marx and Christ
The Blue Guide to West Germany
A Calendar of Saints
Castile
A Children's Bible
Dare to be wise: A History of the Manchester Grammar School
The Gateway to France
A Guide to the Dordogne
A Guide to Tuscany
Italy: the Hilltowns
Languedoc
Life and Food in the Dordogne
The Loire
Martin Niemöller
Normandy
Oberammergau and the Passion Play
Provence and the Côte d'Azur
The Rhine
Ritualism and Politics in Victorian Britain
Rome
Secrets of Mount Sinai
Umbria
The Way of St James
Weekend Cities

Venice & the Veneto

James Bentley

AURUM PRESS

First published 1992 by Aurum Press Limited,
10 Museum Street, London WC1A 1JS
Copyright © 1992 by James Bentley

Map by Chartwell
Decorative illustration by Joy FitzSimmons

A catalogue record for this book is available from
the British Library

ISBN 1 85410 231 1

1   3   5   7   9   10   8   6   4   2
1993   1995   1996   1994   1992

Typeset by Action Typesetting Ltd, Gloucester
Printed in Great Britain by Hartnolls Ltd, Bodmin

Contents

General map of the Veneto

0 |————————————————————| 50 kms

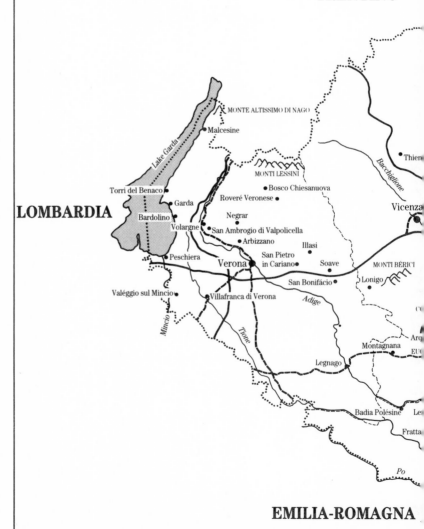

TRENTINO

MONTE ALTISSIMO DI NAGO

• Malcesine

Lake Garda

Bacchiglione

• Thien

MONTI LESSINI

• Bosco Chiesanuova

Torri del Benaco •

Roveré Veronese •

Vicenza

LOMBARDIA

• Garda

Negrar

Bardolino •

Volargne • San Ambrogio di Valpolicella

• Arbizzano

Illasi

Peschiera •

San Pietro
in Cariano •

Soave •

MONTI BÉRICI

Verona

San Bonifácio •

• Lonigo

Valéggio sul Mincio •

Villafranca di Verona

Adige

Mincio

Tione

Montagnana

Arq

EU

Legnago

Badia Polésine   Le

Fratta

Po

EMILIA-ROMAGNA

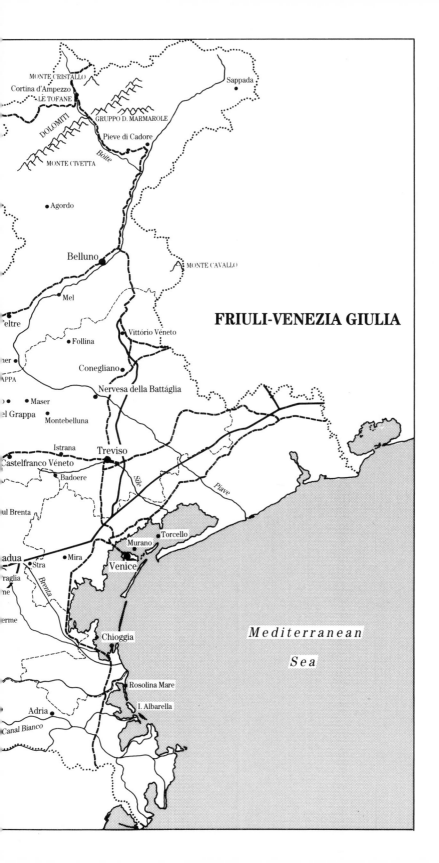

Acknowledgments

My thanks are due first of all to Dottore Emilio Tommasi, Director of the Italian State Tourist Office in London. I am particularly grateful for the immense trouble taken on my behalf by his colleague Signor Eugenio Magnani, and for the kind help also of Signor Paolo Martini.

In Italy I was aided by the staff of the Tourist Boards of Rovigo and Verona, to whom I offer my thanks. Signor Albino Pizzolato and his colleagues at the Azienda di Promozione Turistica of Treviso, as well as Dottore Enzo di Biasi, Director General of the Azienda di Promozione Turistica of Venice, also gave me much help.

I must also thank Prof. Francesco La Valle, of the Azienda di Promozione Turistica, Via Santa Caterina 258, Asolo, and his colleagues Signora Katia Barbisan and Signor Ennio Bittante. At Asolo too I was welcomed and much helped by the General Manager of the Hotel Villa Cipriani, Signor Giuseppe Kamenar.

Signor Aldo Gianetti, President of the Associazione Jesolana Albergatori, Lido di Jesolo, gave me hospitality and rightly pointed out that the immaculate beaches and hotels of that spot are perfect for those who wish to visit Venice in summer without the hassle of

Acknowledgments

actually staying in that inevitably crowded city.

Finally, let me acknowledge the aid of Jennifer Paton, Marketing Director of the Magic of Italy, 227 Shepherd's Bush Road, London W6 7AS.

Preface

In the fourteenth and early fifteenth centuries a group of powerful city states in northern Italy threw in their lot with the republic of Venice as a measure of self-protection against their enemies. The territories they controlled constitute today's Veneto. Their foresight enabled great families to flourish, promoting art and literature, architecture and music, bequeathing to us a superb legacy.

Apart from Venice herself, the major towns and cities with which this book concerns itself are Belluno, Padua, Rovigo, Treviso, Verona and Vicenza. In their varied fashions, each is an unspoilt gem. Belluno offers the best approach to the Dolomites, with their lakes, peaks and ski resorts, but it is entrancing in its own right, with a cathedral built by Tullio Lombardo in the late fifteenth century and its campanile added only in the eighteenth century. At the opposite end of the valley in which it lies is Feltre, its ancient gates protecting each entrance to the medieval main street.

Padua attracted and commissioned the works of such masters as Giotto, Donatello and Titian, and it was the birthplace of the

Renaissance artist Andrea Mantegna, who has left his own mark on the city. Galileo came here as a teacher; the city laid out the first university botanical gardens in Europe; and the university's anatomical theatre, built in 1594, can still be seen. Apart from its own fine architecture (the vast church of Santa Giustina, the intricate narrow streets, the Salone or city tribunal), the environs of Padua are also enticing: the spas of the Euganean hills; the villa at Luvigliano; the gardens of Valsanzibio; the abbey at Praglia.

Two tall defensive towers still rise in Rovigo, all that remains of its former fortress. They defend two palaces, one built by Biagio Rossetti, the other by Michele Sanmicheli, as well as the late sixteenth-century rotunda and the eighteenth-century cathedral. In its turn Rovigo stands sentinel over the Po delta, a landscape of isolated farms, of canals, locks and reed-built fishermen's huts, which has now become a nature reserve.

Treviso, on the River Sile, describes itself as the town of poets, but it was also the home of the Venetian painter Lorenzo Lotto, and the young Titian painted an 'Annunciation' for its cathedral. Though surrounded by hostile-looking walls, water-lapped Treviso is a homelier town than most in the Veneto, a virtue matched by the gentleness of the surrounding hills and such towns as arcaded Conegliano and complex Vittório Véneto, as well as Asolo, which so entranced Pietro Bembo, Robert Browning and Eleonora Duse.

Verona is most celebrated for its Roman arena, but its aspect is above all defensive, expressed in the battlements and turrets of the Castelvecchio bridge and the castle of San Pietro, which defends the bend of the River Adige. The streets of medieval Verona still follow the pattern laid down earlier by the Romans. Its hinterland includes such diverse treats as the intimate sanctuary of the Madonna del Frassino at Peschiera, the fortified wine town of Soave, the range of hills separating the valley of the Adige from Lake Garda, and Caprino Veronese, which each August devotes itself to motor rallies. And fourteen kilometres from Verona the Valpolicella region centres on the village of San Pietro in Cariano.

Vicenza, with its garland of gardens and green hills, is supremely
the city of Palladio, who created not only its villas but also its
uniquely inventive theatre. In this book I try not to allow his
achievement to blur the importance of what came before: the
triumphal columns proclaiming the glorious history of the town;
the legacy of the architect Lorenzo da Bologna; the masterpieces
in the church of Santa Corona (Giovanni Bellini's 'Baptism of Jesus';
Paolo Veronese's 'Adoration of the Magi'). Here, as elsewhere, my
aim is to draw attention to the way this architectural legacy works
today, with the arcades of the central square complementing the
shades of the market stalls in protecting shoppers and stallholders
from the glare of the sun. As for the environs of Vicenza, probably
the name of the animated town of Bassano del Grappa best
encapsulates their charm, combining the adopted title of the artist
Jacopo Bassano with the name of a particularly strong alcoholic
spirit.

The history of the Veneto, where ancient Rome continually
mingles its legacy with later ages, is interwoven with other less
obvious themes. Among these is the importance of water – plain
enough in the case of Venice and the Venetian beaches, but also
recurring in the lagoons, the marshes and Lake Garda, down to
whose Venetan border slope gardens, vineyards and rows of
cypresses. At Treviso the Rivers Sile and Botteniga flow through
the town in a series of canals, which run beside the houses and turn
the wheels of the old mills. In the Po delta, Albarella has developed
as a paradise of 600 hectares of lagoons, woodlands and beaches
in a climate where Mediterranean vegetation flourishes. And in many
spots water bubbles up to the earth's surface to create the beneficially
hot mud that has been exploited by numerous spas.

In writing about this countryside, and these cities and towns, my
plan has been to bring to life those who lived here in the past and
who often described these spots themselves. Petrarch's home still
stands at Arquà Petrarca. The incomparable Palladio was proud
enough to describe his own architecture. Byron's *Childe Harold*
proved so potent a guide book that it inspired Baedeker to found

his celebrated series. Henry James set *The Aspern Papers* at the Palazzo Cappello, Venice. As for the famous villas of the Veneto, where earlier fortresses were replaced by elegant country houses, any twentieth-century guide to the Veneto must evoke the men and women who lived in them, the vision of the past in the present that inspired them to build, and the ethos that infuses their gardens.

Another major aspect of the Veneto is its castles and fortified towns, a theme anchored in this book by visits to such places as Este, Montagnana and Monsélice, to speak only of the region of Padua; as well as to the former strongholds of Asolo and Castelfranco Véneto in the Treviso region; to Soave and Villafranca outside Verona; and to Cittadella near Vicenza. Behind the creation of these fortified towns lies a rich history. As the name Villafranca indicates, those who built them needed to attract men and women to live inside them who were free from any feudal obligations. And the chequerboard plan of walled Cittadella is unmatched outside the elliptical fortified towns of south-west France (with which it is exactly contemporary).

The town of Soave and the name Valpolicella have already brought to mind two distinguished wines, and on the shores of Lake Garda stands Bardolino, which brings to mind yet another. A major thread throughout this book is the varied gastronomy of the region, one which self-evidently includes fish but is also based on *polenta*, on the high-quality hams of the Bérici hills near Vicenza and on humble cheeses. This continually surprising cuisine is not the creation of great chefs and houses, but has developed as an integral part of the conditions of life of ordinary people throughout the centuries.

It is also impossible not to be struck by the spirituality of this region. The Veneto is a land not only of great churches but also of countless sanctuaries. Some of these were built as a thanksgiving for the return of peace, or because a community had survived the plague. Wherever miracles seemed to have occurred, centres of pilgrimage developed and houses of God (for example, that dedicated to the Madonna del Pilastrello at Lendinara, or the spectacularly sited sanctuary of the Madonna della Corona at

Spiazza di Monte Baldo, near Lake Garda) were built to accommodate the pilgrims. In recounting legends and stories, one can begin to understand how these sometimes seemingly naive beliefs can still today retain their powerful grip on people's imaginations.

They are part of the folklore of the Veneto, and folklore is another strand in this book. At Galzigano, for example, each October the Madonna del Rosario is paraded through the streets to celebrate her help in the victory of the Christian armies over the Turks at the Battle of Lepanto in 1571. Then donkeys race in the streets, after which a page in sixteenth-century costume carries a cushion bearing the vanquished Sultan's sword, followed by the donkey that won the previous year's race. Apart from its February carnival, the *Regata Storica*, Venice's most popular festival is the mid-July night of the Redentore, a thank-offering for its salvation from the plague. And many towns in the Veneto organize *palio* races. Feltre celebrates its 1404 union with Venice with such a race, while each February outside the walls of San Zeno Maggiore in the city of Verona fourteen armed horsemen in medieval costume and seven archers (representing the seven districts of the city) compete together.

These festivals encompass not only history and religion but also many of the other elements that recur in the following pages (for instance food and wine: allegorical floats annually trundle through the streets of Soave to rejoice that the vintage has been gathered; at Chioggia during the week-long August fish *sagra*, street stalls fry fresh fish, while the fishermen race against each other in their colourfully-sailed boats; and another gastronomical treat occurs on the first Sunday in June when Maróstica hosts its annual cherry festival).

The heritage of the Veneto is thus astonishingly rich. The region has no fewer than 164 galleries of fine art to complement its architectural legacy. The fecund patrimony of the Veneto ranges from ancient Rome through the baroque to the monuments of our own century, and much of it can be relished simply by walking the streets of its towns and cities. Even the appearance and dialect of the people vary from region to region. Because of its diversity, the many strands of its history and culture, and its varied landscapes and townscapes, the Veneto is not a seamless robe so much as a glittering, enticing patchwork quilt.

James Bentley
APRIL 1992

La Serenissima

'Never have I touched the skirts of so celestial a place,' wrote Elizabeth Barrett Browning on her arrival in Venice in 1851.

The beauty of the architecture, the silver trails of water up between all that gorgeous colour and carving, the enchanting silence, the moonlight, the music, the gondolas – I mix it all up together, and maintain that nothing is like it, nothing equal to it, not a second Venice in the world.

Interlaced marble; brick and flaking stucco; gilded churches; St Mark's square with its musicians and colonnades; quieter squares shaded by magnificent churches; basilicas and palaces lapped by canals; markets nestling in alleyways and beside bridges; melancholy corners and glittering museums – all these constitute a city celebrated in literature and art and, as far as the first goes, curiously enough in English literature above all. Edward Gibbon may have regarded Venice with disgust, but later writers more than made up for the slur.

Byron and Shelley also swam here, even in the Grand Canal, which in subsequent years became a symbol of the dangerous pollution that has attacked the city (and inspired Thomas Mann's novella *Death in Venice*). These canals almost proved the undoing of another Briton. George Eliot, on her marriage to Henry Lewis, was determined to honeymoon here. Alas, Lewis's first marital night with the formidable blue-stocking proved more than he had bargained for, and he leapt from their hotel window and had to be fished (happily, still alive) out of the canal.

And, of course, Venice has not been without her own celebrated writers, among the first Marco Polo, who wrote up his sometimes fantastic, often accurate voyages as a prisoner of Genoa. But the eighteenth century saw the blossoming of Venetian literature, in the dramas of Carlo Goldoni and the equally dramatic (and possibly equally imaginary) memoirs of Giacomo Casanova. Three hundred or so paces north of St Mark's square, behind the church of Santa Maria Formosa, you can vividly appreciate the periwigged life of Goldoni's Venice by savouring the genre paintings of his friend Pietro Longhi, whose characters (best seen in the eighteenth-century Galleria Querini-Stampalia) bustle like mannequins among the streets and squares of contemporary Venice.

This taste for extravagant literature undoubtedly helped to make Venice one of the key centres in the development of Italian opera. In 1613 Claudio Monteverdi, who was born in Cremona and had already written his first opera *Orfeo*, settled in Venice as organist and maestro di cappella at San Marco. Here he continued to write entrancing operas as well as church music and madrigals, culminating in his *Il Ritorno d'Ulisse in patria* and his *L'Incoronazione di Poppea* of 1642. Dying the following year, he was buried in the church of the Frari, having seen no fewer than three opera houses rise in his adopted city.

In the next century such concert halls proved far from sufficient, and theatres and churches were pressed into serving the Venetian passion for music, a passion ministered to, among others, by the baroque master Antonio Vivaldi, who was born here in 1678. Ordained in 1708 (and known as the 'red priest' because of the colour of his hair), Vivaldi became music teacher at the Ospedale della Pietà. Alongside his 450 concerti, forty-six concerti grossi, twenty-three symphonies and two oratorios, he left more than forty operas. Today the church of San Giovanni in Bragora proudly displays the baptismal register in which is inscribed the name of this musician, who died in penury. Giorgio Massari designed the church of the Pietà (Santa Maria della Pietà), on the Riva degli Schiavone, where in his heyday Vivaldi flourished, a church frescoed after the composer's death by the stunning Giambattista Tiepolo himself.

Venetians still love music, in their own curious fashion. On my first visit there I went to hear one of the (several) farewell concert tours of the celebrated pianist Alfred Cortot. Between each piece, no one in the audience fell silent until Cortot had begun to play again; yet the crowd enthusiastically applauded each work, pressing for more and more encores until the pianist played Brahms's 'Cradle Song' and then crept off the stage.

Another recurrent image is of St Mark's square inundated with water. The cry 'Venice in Peril' instantly tugs at the heart-strings. Is the city any more in peril now than it always has been? 'This Venice, which was a haughty, invincible, magnificent Republic for nearly fourteen hundred years,' commented Mark Twain in 1869 in his *Innocents Abroad*:

whose armies compelled the world's applause whenever and wherever they battled; whose navies well nigh held dominion of the seas, and whose merchant fleets whitened the remotest oceans with their sails and loaded those piers with the products of every clime, is fallen a prey to poverty, neglect, and melancholy decay.

Dogged by erosion, subject to floods, at the mercy of freak waves, polluted, its pillars and foundations corroded and pitted, Venice ought long ago to have sunk beneath the sea. Yet when last in apparently acute danger, its thousand-year-old foundations were examined by architects and other specialists and discovered to be still firmly immobile.

Yet anyone who walks its narrow streets, explores its hidden squares and sails its canals cannot help marvelling at the survival of such a seemingly fragile city. Even its architecture is less substantial than it appears at first sight. The stones of Venice often consist of a brick building cunningly concealed under a thin skin of marble. And lichen does fester on its ancient walls.

Historically, too, Venice has survived a precarious development. Even the story of its legendary connection with St Mark exudes peril. Having embarked from Aquileia for Alexandria, his vessel was battered by a sudden storm on the Adriatic coast and the saint was obliged to take refuge on an island in what was to become the lagoon of Venice. There a heavenly voice addressed him: 'Pax tibi, Marce evangelista meus' ('Peace be with you, my evangelist Mark'). The message bore a double significance. First, that St Mark was approaching a martyr's death. Second, that his body would eventually find rest on this island. So the apostle continued as far as Alexandria, where pagans killed him and threw his corpse in unconsecrated ground. There it lay for seven centuries, until in 828 two Venetian merchants stole the holy relic and transported the saint's bones back to Venice.

Even then the spot was inhabited only by a few fisherfolk and salt workers. Their home was a bizarre conglomeration of islands and the 'terra firma'. Their livelihoods and lives were continually threatened by barbarians and by the Lombards. Yet slowly they and their homeland prospered, becoming a major support of the Byzantine empire, which Constantine the Great had based in Constantinople in AD 331. So great a maritime power did Venice become that in 1204 she supplanted Constantinople as capital of the empire. To rule the Venetians, dukes, or doges, were appointed by Venice's mistress from the early eighth century. Their lives were initially precarious, the first one, Orso Ipato, meeting his death at the hand of an assassin.

Successive doges remained the object of hatred and envy. Great Venetian families disputed the right to accord the title and its power to one of their members. The Contarini family supplied eight doges; the Mocenigo family seven; the Morosini four; and the Corner family another four. They numbered themselves among the great ones of the world, and under their sway Venice managed to fend off her enemies while developing as a dominant naval power. The doges eventually declared themselves Dukes of Dalmatia, and the Holy Roman Emperor had no choice but to agree to their new presumption. Venetians took part in the Crusades, thereby enriching themselves and increasing their international sway. Thoughout the eleventh century their armies withstood the depradations of the Normans and in 1085 finally freed the Adriatic from their assaults.

In the meantime, Venetian merchants were systematically establishing their city as the major hub of trade between the Western world and the Orient. Spices, cotton, precious metals, corn, wood, perfume, iron and bronze goods travelled east and west through her port. Yet never did the city avoid anxieties and troubles. Her favoured name, La Serenissima, in no way describes the normal state of affairs in Venice. In the second half of the twelfth century Frederick Barbarossa menaced her stability. She saw off the threat. In 1159 the papacy was in dispute. Venice supported the legitimacy of Alexander III, and Barbarossa the anti-Pope Octavius. Alexander triumphed and, to the glory of Venice, Barbarossa and the Pope were reconciled on 24 July 1177, beneath the porch of St Mark's cathedral.

By now Venetians were ruthless in their pursuit of wealth and in the aggrandisement of their city, aided by their superb fleet. During the fourth Crusade her vassals pillaged Constantinople, bringing home among many treasures the horses that now adorn the basilica of San Marco. Her ships dominated lands as far off as Armenia, Egypt and the Crimea. Byzantium was now in truth her vassal, and not vice versa. Still she had no peace. The Genoese in particular resented her hegemony and took care to support the last vestiges of Byzantine power. In 1379 their troops managed to penetrate the outskirts of La Serenissima, before the Venetian soldiers defeated them.

Such dangers persuaded the Venetians to conquer (and thus in a sense to create) the stupendously attractive province of Italy which forms the subject of this book. The cities of her hinterland, particularly Padua and Verona, were ever-ready to hinder Venice's trade with the rest of Europe. Doge Steno decided to bring them and the rest of the 'terra firma' under Venetian sway. His policy was continued by Doge T. Mocenigo and, above all, by Doge Francesco Foscari (who ruled from 1423 to 1457). At Verona the ruling Scaliger family met its defeat. So did the Carraresi of Verona, as well as the Hungarians, the Austrians and the Dukes of Milan.

Venice would undoubtedly have spread her hegemony further into Italy but for the fall of Constantinople at the hands of Sultan Mahomet II in 1453. The Ottoman empire now overwhelmed most of Venice's eastern empire. Her trading power began abruptly to slip away when Vasco da Gama discovered a route to India around the Cape in 1497. Weakened abroad, Venice was forced to cede many of her Italian conquests. She withdrew not into herself but into a far more defensible and thus profitable situation. The loss of many of her colonies paradoxically resulted in a new efflorescence at home. This was the era when the Venetians built in their own city the superb late Gothic and Renaissance buildings that are today still reflected in the city's canals. The canals themselves were enormously improved. And in the sixteenth century Venice attracted artists of the calibre of Titian, Tintoretto and Veronese, while her nobles and doges began the habit of building themselves summer villas in the hinterland.

The Turks, the Austrians and the French continued to threaten the city, and the Venetian coffers were drained by the need for incessant defensive struggles. In the eighteenth century her leaders attempted a policy of neutrality, preferring to be regarded as a negligible power rather than a great one. But her maritime trade was drying up. Venice was obliged to ally herself with the Austrians and then, on 12 May 1797, the last of her doges, Ludovico Manin, abdicated in the face of the assault of Napoleon Bonaparte. Five years later William Wordsworth movingly lamented the fall of the republic:

> Once did She hold the gorgeous east in fee;
> And was the safeguard of the west.

Napoleon was an innovator in town planning as well as much else. Was his intrusion beneficial for Venice? Austere architects would say no; most visitors would disagree. Bonaparte re-ordered St Mark's square, laying the foundations for what Venetians today describe as the finest open-air café in the world. (They politely ignore remarks that it might also be the most expensive.) The architects point out that to do so Bonaparte ordered the destruction of Sansovino's church of San Geminiano, replacing it with the monotonous colonnades of the Fabbrica Nuova.

In the name of progress, Venice thenceforth suffered further attacks on its architectural patrimony. When the railway arrived, its engineers destroyed a convent and a church by Palladio. Only in the twentieth century did the authorities of La Serenissima regain their senses, rightly (in my view) refusing permission for planned monstrosities designed by Frank Lloyd Wright and the odious Le Corbusier.

After Napoleon, the Austrians again took control of the once-proud city. In the revolutionary year of 1848 Daniele Manin proclaimed a republic here, but it could not last. Austria once more controlled Venice until, in 1866, she became free again by voting to become part of the new Italian nation.

The artistic patrimony of Venice reflects this long history. Byzantine architecture, that style which prospered under the might of Western Roman emperors ruling from Constantinople, continually emerges in Venice and its adjoining cities. Until malaria decimated its population, the island of Torcello far outstripped the rest of the Veneto in trade and wealth. The cathedral of Santa Maria Assunta, Torcello (probably the oldest building in the whole region), was begun in the seventh century, though its present form dates from the ninth to the eleventh centuries, and brilliant mosaicists continued to decorate it until the thirteenth. Its apse is adorned with a superb mosaic of the Madonna, while the other glory of the building is a mosaic of the Last Judgement. Another gem is the little church of Santa Fosca, built on the island in the thirteenth century, its octagonal plan based on Oriental models.

Without taking a boat trip to Torcello, most visitors savour Byzantine Venice simply by visiting San Marco, whose basilica was begun in the eleventh century during the reign of Doge Domenico Contarini. Its architectural inspiration came directly from Constantinople, from the church of the Holy Apostles, which served as the imperial mausoleum. On the altar of the Blessed Virgin in the left transept, for example, is a much venerated Byzantine icon of the Madonna Nicopeai (which means 'the Madonna who gives victory'), brought here from Constantinople in 1204. Byzantine elements also long survived in the architecture of the palaces lining Venice's canals, for example the Palazzo Dona della Madonetta and the Palazzo Dona, which sit side-by-side along the Grand Canal.

Gothic Venice owes much to the religious orders, in particular the Dominicans and the Franciscans. Legend has it that in 1230 Doge Jacopo Tiepolo had a dream of doves and flowers, fluttering above and falling on to a square in Venice, while a voice rang out, 'This is the spot I have chosen for my preachers.' On waking, the doge sped to the senate and persuaded the city fathers to endow a church there for the Dominicans. On this spot rose the monastery, hospice and basilica of Santi Giovanni e Paolo, which today everyone calls San Zanipolo.

The Franciscans, who arrived in Venice in the early thirteenth century, at first inhabited a small chapel before following the example of the Dominicans in building their church out of spare brick, only occasionally enlivened with lacy stonework. And, as with San Zanipolo, the dedication of this early fourteenth-century basilica, Santa Maria Gloriosa Dei, is universally contracted into a nickname, the Frari.

Such fastidious Gothic building contrasts remarkably with the flamboyance of the secular Gothic of the era, particularly some of the palaces along the Grand Canal. The Ca' d'Oro is the best known, built between 1421 and 1436. Its architects were Matteo Raverti, Giovanni Buon and his son Bartolommeo. (Today the palace serves as an art gallery, displaying a 'St Sebastian' by Mantegna and Titian's 'Venus before a Mirror'.)

Other Gothic palaces along the Grand Canal include the fifteenth-century Palazzo Erizzo, the Palazzo Pesaro Rava of the same date (which stands next door to the Ca' d'Oro) and (the next palace along the canal) the late fourteenth-century Palazzo Morosini Sagredo with its refined loggia. On the opposite side of the Grand Canal, notable Gothic palaces are the early fifteenth-century Ca' Foscari, now the home of the Venetian university of economics and commerce, and the Palazzo Loredan dell'Ambasciatore, so named because the Austrian ambassador lived here in the eighteenth century. Yet more Gothic palaces have been transformed into luxury hotels, especially the Palazzo Pisani Gritti (now the Hotel Gritti), while the Venetian tourist office is situated in the fifteenth-century Ca' Giustinian.

Renaissance palaces also abound. The art of Tuscan Renaissance first makes its appearance in Venice in the exquisitely proportioned Palazzo Corner della Ca' Grande, which Jacopo Sansovino designed alongside the Grand Canal for one of the sons of the stupendously rich Venetian merchant Giorgio Corner. Rusticated walls delineate the first storey, while the brackets framing the mezzanine windows derive directly from Michelangelo's Palazzo Medici in Florence.

The arrival in 1530 of Sansovino (his real name was Jacopo Tatti), who lived and worked here until 1570, in truth marked a major development in Venetian architecture. Sansovino was a Florentine who had honed his talents in Rome under the tutelage of Raphael and Michelangelo. He ought to have found

his permanent niche in Rome when Giulio de' Medici became
Pope Clement VII in 1523. But the sack of Rome by imperial
troops four years later scattered the artists of the papal court
throughout Italy. Aged forty-three, Sansovino chose to make his
home in Venice. His high Renaissance artistry changed the face
of the city.

To him Venice owes, above all, the design and building of
the Libreria, opposite the Doges' Palace. Inspired by antiquity,
Sansovino's aim was to create here a fanciful replica of the Roman
forum (and inspired by Sansovino others, such as Vincenzo
Scamozzi in 1582, realized this dream).

This blend of Byzantine, Gothic and Renaissance architecture
is what makes sailing along the Grand Canal irresistible; but the
combination continually recurs elsewhere in Venice. And the first
evidence of Renaissance architecture in Venice (a phenomenon
that emerged some fifty years after its flowering in Florence)
appears not alongside the Grand Canal but in the shape of the gate
of the Arsenal, designed by Antonio Gambello in 1460. Today
this gate fronts all that remains of a mighty citadel, mentioned
by Dante in the XXIst canto of his *Inferno*. From the Arsenal,
the Venetian fleet sailed to conquer the known world. And in
the late seventeenth century Admiral Francesco Morosini brought
from Greece the playful white marble lions that still guard the
entrance to the stern, crenellated brick fortress and towers.

Before Sansovino, the Renaissance style had already appeared
in Venice through the work of one great family of architects.
Pietro Lombardo was born in 1435 and died in 1515. His son
Tullio, and his contemporary Mauro Coducci, embroidered and
enhanced the tradition which Pietro had brought, as his name
implies, from Lombardy (though he had worked with, and learned
from, the Tuscan genius Donatello at Padua).

Pietro Lombardo's work deliciously crosses the borderline
between the Gothic and Renaissance styles. The first sight of
his Santa Maria Nuova is, to say the least, startling. On the
Grand Canal his masterpiece is the Palazzo Dario, a triumph of

delicate pink and white marble built in 1487. His finest Venetian church is Santa Maria dei Miracoli, built between 1481 and 1489. As for Mauro Coducci, his most acclaimed building is Santa Maria Formosa, completed in 1492, though San Giovanni Crisostomo (built between 1497 and 1504) runs it a close second. Coducci also built another exquisite Renaissance church for Venice, this one in 1469 and on the melancholy island of San Michele, where lie buried such Russian geniuses as Igor Stravinsky and Serge Diaghilev.

Thenceforth a series of brilliant architects continued to enhance the city. Giorgio Spavento, who died in 1509, created both the Fondaco dei Tedeschi (a warehouse for German merchants near the Rialto bridge) and the church of San Salvador. Michele Sanmicheli, whose career straddled the fifteenth and sixteenth centuries (he was born in 1484, dying in 1559), left to Venice the Palazzi Grimani and Gussoni-Grimani, both on the Grand Canal.

Palladio also contributed his genius to the city. Oddly enough, here he was commissioned to build not villas but churches. The church of the Redentore, San Giorgio Maggiore, part of San Pietro di Castello, San Francesco della Vigna and the cloister of the basilica of the Frari testify to his refined response to ancient Roman forms. His personal preference for the play of light and shade, his refusal to allow statues and superfluous ornaments to disfigure the tops of walls, and his delight in Florentine cupolas (though he was born a Venetian) repeatedly identify Palladio's work in Venice.

One of his most audacious façades, on the church of San Francesco della Vigna not far from the Arsenal, fronts a church built by Sansovino, who died before its completion. Inspired by Greco-Roman temples, Palladio designed a portico with colonnades, over which rises the temple-like architrave. This church houses a dazzling display of classical paintings and sculpture. Veronese's 'Sacra Conversazione' dates from 1562. Paintings by Palma the Younger hang beside statues sculpted by Antonio and

Tullio Lombardo. Alessandro Vittoria designed an altar whose sculpted saints represent Roch, Sebastian and Antony Abbot. From an earlier age is a glowing fifteenth-century painting of the Madonna and child by Fra Antonio da Negroponte.

San Francesco della Vigna is one of the last classical churches in Venice, although another of Palladio's gifts to the city was the rebuilding of its first cathedral, San Pietro in Castello, whose late fifteenth-century campanile is by Coducci. Then the baroque breaks through. The spectacular forest of statues on the church of the Salute by Baldassare Longhena (1598–1682), a Venetian-born disciple of Scamozzi, clearly renounces Palladio's austerity, even though its Roman fronton still speaks of antiquity. Its massive cupola announces the arrival of Venetian baroque. Longhena relished monumental forms, as his palaces, the Ca' Rezzonico and the Ca' Pesaro (today the city's museum of modern art), proclaim.

One of his pupils, Giuseppe Sardi (1630–99), continued this baroque vitality in the façades of the churches of Santa Maria del Giglio and of the Scalzi (whose basic plan was Longhena's). And the delirious façade of San Moisè, built between 1632 and 1688, outdoes them all in baroque frenzy.

Throughout these centuries a galaxy of other artists added to the glory of these superb buildings. On my first visit to Venice, ravished by paintings that I had previously encountered only in inadequate reproductions, I learnt that much great art here is concealed in the crannies of churches and convents. Sail to Torcello or relish the mosaics of San Marco, and you are enchanted by the art of Byzantium. The spirit of Byzantium lived on in the work of the Vivarini family, who were mosaicists and glass-makers. Antonio Vivarini, who worked throughout most of the fifteenth century, has left us the superb 'Coronation of the Virgin Mary' that adorns the church of San Pantaleone on the island of Murano. Around 1450 he and his younger brother Bartolomeo painted a glittering triptych for the church of Santa Maria Formosa.

Murano is also the best place to enjoy Venetian glassware. The first glass-blowers' guild was established in Venice in 1224, and its members moved to the island of Murano in 1291. It remains the home of their descendants. Refugees from Byzantium swelled their numbers in the mid-fifteenth century. They aimed at creating clear glassware that resembled rock crystal and, having achieved this by the sixteenth century, turned their minds to the technique of adding colour and gilt to their exquisite vessels. By this time, too, the city's craftsmen were also creating masterpieces of majolica.

The achievement of the Vivarini is eclipsed by that of the Bellini family – Jacopo (who lived from 1400 to 1470) and his two sons, Gentile and Giovanni. The three artists specialized in Madonnas, without ever reducing their works to simple fifteenth-century formulae. Their achievement, in my view, was in part due to their skill in expressing nuances of emotion by means of delicate colours. But the older son, Gentile, also discovered another fruitful source of patronage: the depiction of those Venetian confraternities known as *scuoli*. His friend Vittore Carpaccio frequently helped him in these lucrative commissions.

As for the younger artist, Giovanni Bellini (who was called Giambellino), his greatest accomplishment was to set up an artists' workshop in which worked such masters as Giorgione and Titian – with the consequence that the heritage of this man, who died aged eighty-six in 1516, dominated Venetian painting throughout the fifteenth century and for the first part of the sixteenth.

One reason for this dominance must be the diverse artistic influences that Giambellino managed to blend into one. He knew and learned from the German genius Albrecht Dürer. Byzantium and the late Italian Gothic inspired him. So did his brother-in-law Mantegna, the greatest Paduan artist of the era. Flemish painting, at the time led by Van Eyck, also lent its skills to Giovanni Bellini through its intermediary Antonello da Messina.

Can we still detect a technical (and spiritual) arrogance in his work? In the church of the Madonna dell'Orto, for example, Bellini created a Madonna which seems to present itself as a deliberate rival to the miracle-working statue of the Virgin from which this church derives its name. 'Madonna dell'Orto' means the Madonna of the Garden, a reference to a statue of the Virgin Mary, sculpted in stone in the fourteenth century by Giovanni di Santi. He placed the statue in his garden, and was surprised to find numerous pilgrims venerating the image he had created. In 1377 the Madonna was solemnly placed inside this church. Today it sits alongside Bellini's image of the Virgin Mary. And others followed Bellini's presumption. In 1556 Tintoretto painted his 'Presentation of the Virgin Mary in the Temple' for the church. Tintoretto may well regret swamping the glory of these lovely paintings with the gigantic 'Last Judgement' he also painted for this same church.

Giambellino never allowed the human form to overwhelm the divine in his art. His paintings depict human beings as shadowy forms beside the gods and goddesses. Vittore Carpaccio was a more exuberant humanist. Still giving his paintings religious titles and adopting religious themes (the 'Legend of St Ursula', the 'Miracle of the Holy Cross'), he nevertheless depicted splendid Venetian tableaux, with the sails of merchant vessels swelling in the breeze, the citizens richly clad, the architecture sumptuous.

As for Tiziano Vecellio, whom we know as Titian, one day he dropped a brush on the floor in the presence of the Emperor Charles V. The emperor picked it up for him, with the words, 'Titian is worthy of being served by Caesar.' Titian's life spanned most of the sixteenth century. (He died of the plague in 1576.) Born in the Dolomite village of Pieve di Cadore, the artist gained instant recognition in 1515 with his 'Sacred and profane love'. Drawn first to Padua, Titian was soon fêted in Venice herself. To savour his greatness, find inside the church of the Frari his superb 'Assumption'.

Like every artist of his epoch, Titian taught pupils who worked on his canvases. For this reason Venice possesses a unique painting, in the church of San Salvatore (which stands between St Mark's square and the Rialto bridge). It depicts the Annunciation, and was painted when Titian was ninety-four years old. To insist that he alone had created this lovely work of art, Titian inscribed it with a double verb: 'Titianus fecit fecit'.

One of his pupils, Jacopo Robusti, took the nickname Tintoretto (since he was the son of a dyer). Titian jealously hated his brilliant follower, and made it difficult for Tintoretto to gain commissions. Initially Tintoretto exhibited his work in the streets, executing a series of canvases for the church of the Madonna dell'Orto free of charge. His career took off in the mid-sixteenth century, when he painted a group of canvases for the Scuola di San Rocco, where you can compare at leisure both Titian and his feared pupil. Titian painted a splendid 'Annunciation' for the *scuola*. Scholars dispute whether he or Giorgione painted a miracle-working picture of Jesus carrying his cross.

Then, in 1564, a competition was arranged to decide who should paint the walls of the *scuola*. Artists of the stature of Andrea Schiavone, Paolo Veronese, Francesco Salviati and the Zuccari were among the contestants. Tintoretto won by secretly painting a ceiling, covering it with damask and unveiling it before the judges, with the promise that if they appointed him he would charge them only the cost of his materials for this work of art. The result is that today you can relish nearly forty masterpieces, painted by Tintoretto between 1564 and 1587 (seven years before his death) in this *scuola* dedicated to St Roch, the saint reputed to be best able to protect believers from the plague.

Veronese, who was trumped in the competition by Tintoretto, was born Paolo Caliari in Verona in 1528. Another native of Verona, Bernardo Torlioni, took holy orders and eventually became prior of the convent of San Sebastiano, Venice. Bernardo invited Veronese to decorate the convent church, and this work brought the painter fame and more commissions here, in particular that of decorating the ceiling of the library of San Marco.

In 1562 Veronese was back in Venice, executing paintings for the church of San Giorgio Maggiore. Here one picture brought him criticism from the Holy Office in Rome. His depiction of the Last Supper was deemed far too secular in tone. Why, his judges asked, had he added to the scene of Jesus with his twelve apostles other characters, such as drunken German halbardiers, buffoons and dwarfs? Veronese responded by changing its title to 'The Dinner in the House of Levi'.

It seems fitting that Venice's finest eighteenth-century painter, Giambattista Tiepolo, should have been born in 1696 the son of a ship's captain. His work can be seen at its finest in the ceiling of the Sandi palace, in the frescos that he painted for the Jesuits' church in 1735 and for the church of the Carmini (the Chiesa e Scuola Dei di Santa Maria del Carmelo) eight years later. Titian's sombre, cruel 'Martyrdom of St Lawrence' hangs above the first altar on the left in the Chiesa dei Gesuiti. This ravishing baroque church also houses Tintoretto's 'Ascension of the Blessed Virgin' and works by Palma the Younger (with whose daughter Titian was madly in love), as well as a stunning high altar designed by G. Pozzo and G. Torreto. At the church of the Carmini, Tiepolo's style is infinitely lighter than Titian's. The allegories he frescoed for the *scuola* were done when the artist was in his forties. Alongside his work in the neighbouring church are paintings by Palma the Younger, a 'Nativity' of 1509 by Cima da Conegliano and Lorenzo Lotto's 'St Nicholas in Glory', painted twenty years later.

Tiepolo married the sister of a fellow-painter, Francesco Guardi, who belonged to that group of artists which gave Venice a wider fame by their skill at producing architectural views that were nevertheless also superb works of art. The most celebrated of these artists were Antonio Canal, known as Canaletto, who made several visits to England, where he applied the same technique to views of the Thames; and his nephew Bernardo Bellotto (who, to confuse the lay mind, was also known as Canaletto). Almost all these masters are sumptuously displayed in the

Galleria dell'Accademia. The influence of Byzantium lives on here in the works of Lorenzo and Paolo Veneziano. To Giambellino are devoted two rooms of the gallery, while the rest of the Bellini dynasty overflows elsewhere. Vittore Carpaccio is here represented by his supreme achievement, the 'Legend of St Ursula', in which the architectural and naval details of the painting seem to glorify an idealized Venice as much as the virgin martyr of Cologne. And do not miss one of Titian's last works (maybe his very last), the *Pietà* he painted in 1576 when he was nearly a hundred. Tintoretto, for his part, magnifies Venice by contributing stirring evocations of the legend of St Mark; while Veronese's audacious 'The Dinner in the House of Levi' hangs here and not in the convent of SS Giovanni e Paolo, for which it was painted. Only such special geniuses as Canaletto are strangely absent from the Accademia. Since one cannot overlook Venice through his eyes, it is time to take a walk through the streets and view the city for yourself.

If you start at the main railway station and turn left, you find the church of the Scalzi (Santa Maria di Nazareth degli Scalzi), which stands opposite one of the three bridges spanning the Grand Canal, this one built by Eugenio Miozzi in 1934. Baldassare Longhena, who designed this baroque church in 1656, also had the honour of building the church that stands at the other end of the Grand Canal, Santa Maria della Salute.

The Scalzi were Carmelite friars who went unshod, and one of their number, Fra Giuseppe Pozzo (who lived from 1680 to 1753), was privileged to finish the façade of their church. He took as his theme the triumph of the Virgin Mary. Sculpted on his façade is Jesus, with Eve and Abel on his left and Adam and Cain on his right. Above them in glory is the Virgin, who is surrounded by St Jerome, the virtue Faith, St Batholomew and the virtue Hope (which is fallen and broken). Above this complex is a third group of sculptures: Saints Sebastian, Mary Magdalene, Margaret and John the Baptist.

17

Nearby in Sestier de Cannaregio, the eighteenth-century Palazzo Labbia displays a group of splendid baroque frescos, painted by Tiepolo in the late 1740s on the subject of Cleopatra, which go some way to making up for the loss of his 'Miracle of the Holy House of Loreto', which once adorned the ceiling of the church of the Scalzi and was lost during the First World War when the Austrians shelled Venice. Happily, this privately owned palace opens to the public on Wednesdays, Thursdays and Fridays, though it is best to make prior arrangements for a visit.

Shops selling jewellery, Venetian glass, leather goods, masks, clothing, food and wine line Ria Terrà Lista di Spagna, which runs from the church of the Scalzi to the square of the eighteenth-century church of San Geremia. The masks evoke the gay, sometimes wild festivals of Venice. To ourselves, as heirs of the travellers of yesteryear, they also bespeak those who participated in them long ago, for little has changed. These masks come into their own whenever the Venetians disport themselves, particularly at Carnival. Sometimes, I think, Canaletto, whose paintings of eighteenth-century Italian life so entrance the British, equally inspires the Venetians to adorn themselves for their traditional festivals.

How it must have entranced visitors, when the Venetians always dressed like this, can be gauged from Joseph Addison's record of his stay in Venice at the very start of the eighteenth century. Virtually his whole account concerns the way people dressed. The women wore such high-heeled shoes that when they sank into a gondola they seemed like dwarfs, 'taken down from their wooden scaffolds'. Their petticoats reached up to their armpits. Their sleeves were exceedingly wide, 'shewing their naked arms thro' false sleeves of tiffany'. Addison noted that married women went about in black veils, and he added:

The nobility wear the same colour, but of fine cloth lin'd with taffeta in Summer, with fur of the bellies of squirrells in the Winter, which all put on at a certaine day girt with a girdle emboss'd with silver; the vest not much different from what our Bachelors of Arts weare in Oxford, and a hood of cloth made like a sack, cast over the left shoulder.

Addison saw the doge go by wearing a vest of crimson velvet, with the procurators following in damask, 'very stately'. He was astonished at:

the strange variety of the several nations which were seen every day in the streets and piazzas; Jews, Turks, Armenians, Persians, Moores, Greekes, Sclavonians, some with their tatgets and boucklers, and all in their native fashions, negotiating in this famous Emporium, which is allways crowded with strangers.

And so it is in Venice today, save that the costumes sparkle less.

The church of San Geremia is also known as Santa Lucia di Siracusa, since it shelters the uncorrupted corpse of St Lucy, brought here from Syracusa in Sicily, where she was martyred. Today Lucy lies in a glass shrine, displayed to the public. A plaque announces not only her legendary skill at healing eyes but also her continual intercession for the peace of the world.

Beyond the piazza you cross Ponte Guglie and turn left alongside the canal to discover a signpost in Hebrew and Italian directing you to the *Sinagogh*. Until the sixteenth century Venice possessed no ghetto (a word which, since it was coined here, has been attached to every Jewish quarter in every city throughout the world). In earlier times her Jews were dispersed throughout the city. Only in 1527 did the city fathers gather the Jews of Venice in what became known as the *Ghetto Vecchio* (to distinguish the quarter from the *Ghetto Nuovo*).

Since some 5,000 Jews were barricaded in the *Ghetto Vecchio*, they were forced to build higher and higher to house themselves. Obliged to wear yellow hats whenever they ventured elsewhere in Venice, the Jews set up a centre of culture and Rabbinical learning, which disappeared only in the mid-eighteenth century, when exorbitant taxes forced most of them to quit the city that had once been their refuge. The descendants of those who stayed now run shops selling Jewish delicacies and a Jewish bakery. Here are their school and synagogue. Here too is a monument commemorating the 200 Venetian Jews, the 800 Italian Jews and the six million or so others slaughtered by the Nazis. On the school wall a plaque remembers twenty-four Venetian Jews who died fighting for Italy in the First World War.

The Campo di Ghetto Nuovo, a little further north, on an island in the Sestier de Cannaregio beside the Cannaregio canal, has another grim memorial. Seven bronzes by A. Blates depict Jewish suffering in concentration camps between 1943 and 1945. The inscription reads, 'Our memories are your only grave.' In this *campo* are a sixteenth-century synagogue and a Jewish museum.

Beside the synagogue a passageway runs over a canal and down Calle Ghetto Novisimo as far as Rio Terrà Farsetti, where you turn right to follow Calle de Pistor. Here flower, fruit and vegetable shops spill out into the street. Ahead, over another canal bridge, runs Strada Nova, at the end of which rises the church of San Fosca. A medieval church rebuilt in the seventeenth century, it preserves its fifteenth-century campanile and was given a new façade in 1741.

Opposite rises the Renaissance Palazzo Corner, which was built by Sansovino in the mid-sixteenth century. Cross a bridge dedicated to Niccolò Pasquaglio and you will see to your right across the Grand Canal an even finer palace. The Ca' Pesaro is the finest baroque building lining the canal. Created in 1685 by Baldassare Longhena on behalf of Doge Giovanni Pesaro, today it houses the city's museum of modern art. Some of the finest works on show in the Ca' Pesaro seem strangely out of place in Venice, even when one remembers her Austrian connections. Gustav Klimt's disturbing 'Salome' is a case in point. But the splendid works by such masters as Pierre Bonnard, Paul Klee, Vasily Kandinsky, Joan Miró, Raoul Dufy, Giorgio de Chirico and Georges Rouault render the exhibition worthy of the title Galleria Internationale d'Arte Moderna. A display of Japanese and Chinese works rounds off the collection.

One of Venice's showpieces, the Ca' d'Oro, seems reluctant to reveal itself. Walking on along Strada Nova past the sixteenth-century church of San Felice and across another canal bridge, you can easily miss an insignificant notice on your right, pointing down an alleyway to this palace. Matteo Raverti began building the Ca' d'Oro in 1421. It was finished some fifteen years later. Today the palace houses the Galleria Franchetti, an art gallery with works by (among others) Pisanello, Mantegna, Filippo Lippi and Titian. But what strikes the visitor above all is the fantastic tracery of its Gothic façade.

At the end of Strada Nova rises the sixteenth-century church of SS Apostoli, with a campanile of 1672 and, inside, a painting by Tiepolo. On its walls is a signpost, directing you towards the church of Santi Giovanni e Paolo. In fact, the first superb church *en route* turns out to be Santa Maria dei Miracoli. Surrounded by water, this is a magical oddity in Venice. It was built to house a miracle-working image of the Virgin Mary (as its name suggests), which was painted in 1408 by Niccolò di Pietro. So many wax candles and ex-votos were paid for as a result of the Virgin's beneficial ways that by the end of the century a procession of procurators and senators, accompanied by trumpets, pipes, drums and candles, led a concourse of citizens to house the statue in a temporary wooden chapel, draped with a cloth of gold and silver.

After a competition to design a permanent home for the statue had been won by Pietro Lombardo, the present building was begun in the early 1480s. It constitutes Venice's finest piece of Tuscan architecture. Marble was brought here from Pisa and Genoa, and the store was added to by pirates, who lifted more marble from captured vessels. So much money was raised for this building that Santa Maria dei Miracoli became the first church in Venice to be entirely clad in marble, in a multicoloured, streaky pattern that covers the church inside and out. Inside, yellow and dove-grey marble, with red and gold bands, rises to a barrel-vaulted ceiling of painted and gilded wood. Its squares frame portraits of the prophets.

Venice is here well-signposted, and a placard outside the church indicates (for a second time) the way to the magnificent basilica of Santi Giovanni e Paolo. In the church's piazza struts the arrogant equestrian statue of Bartolomeo Colleone, which the Florentine sculptor Andrea del Verrocchio created in 1481 (though after his death in 1488 it was finished by Alessandro Leopardi). Colleone envied the statue of his fellow-*condottiere* Guattamelata, which Donatello had already created in Padua. In Colleone's own statue the steed's nostrils dilate, as do his veins and muscles. Colleone seems to be in a frightful temper, as no doubt befits a military man of his fierce stamp.

The church is flanked by the civic hospital, once a charitable foundation known as the Scuola Grande di San Marco. In the fifteenth century Pietro Lombardo and his son created its marble façade, its perspectives cunningly suggesting three-dimensional views. Later, others added to the façade of the *scuola*, the last to do so being Mauro Coducci, while Sansovino created the long monumental wall which stretches alongside the canal. Its chapel, built two centuries after the *scuola* was founded, is by Scamozzi, and it houses a crucifixion by Veronese and a painting of St Ursula by Tintoretto.

As for the huge Gothic basilica, which was built for the Dominicans, its lovely porch is by Bartolommeo Buon. Inside lie a score of doges, some of them in magnificent tombs. Doge Antonio Venier, who died in 1420, lies over the doorway of the chapel of the Holy Rosary – a chapel in which are found the finest works of art in the basilica: paintings by Veronese. Doge Michele Morosini commissioned for himself the most obtrusive and grandiose tomb. And beside the entrance to the basilica Pietro Lombardo sculpted a still finer tomb for Doge Pietro Mocenigo, while Lombardo's son Tullio designed another with equal elegance for Doge Giovanni Mocenigo. Pietro Lombardo also created a tomb for Doge Nicolai Marcello (on the left of the nave), in which Marcello is borne by four lovely young women representing the cardinal virtues.

Both Palma the Elder and Titian lie buried here, their tombs the work of Vincenzo Scamozzi. And the basilica is also blessed with rococo statues (Saints Albertus Magnus, Thomas Aquinas and Dominic) by Andrea Brustolon. Another bizarre relic, the skin of the Venetian admiral Marco Antonio Bragadin, is displayed in the right-hand aisle of the church. Bragadin had been flayed alive by the Turks after his heroic, but futile, defence of Famagusta in 1571. The Venetians rescued his skin from their traditional enemy in 1656 and brought the relic home.

Yet another useful notice directs you from here to the church of Santa Maria Formosa and the cathedral of San Marco. Antonio Gambello, architect of the Renaissance doorway of the Arsenal, began the present façade of Santa Maria Formosa in 1444, but the main credit for this façade, finished in 1500, must go to Coducci. To one's surprise, the interior is Gothic. Santa Maria Formosa was founded by the Benedictines in the twelfth century, but its name derives from a legendary appearance on this spot in the seventh century of the Blessed Virgin, buxom in form (hence the epithet *formosa*, which means 'ample').

Gothic polyptychs decorate the church's altars. The flowery one on the altar of the chapel of San Tarasio depicts the Virgin Mary flanked by saints, and was created on gilded and sculpted wood by Ludovico da Forli in 1444 and painted by Vivarini da Murano and Giovanni d'Alemagna. Vivarini painted two other polyptychs here, while an earlier altarpiece dating from 1385 is by Stefano da Sant'Agnèse. Giovanni Bellini contributed to this church the altarpiece depicting the Virgin and child surrounded by Saints Peter, Catherine, Lucy and Jerome; Titian painted an 'Addolorata'; Tintoretto was responsible for the 'Birth of St John'; and another 'Virgin with Saints' is by Palma the Elder.

West of this *campo*, by way of the seventeenth-century church of San Lio (whose ceiling was decorated by Tiepolo and whose Giusoni chapel was designed by Pietro Lombardo), you reach Campo San Bartolomeo. In the middle of this square is a nineteenth-century statue, by Antonio del Zotto, of the dramatist Carlo Goldoni, who made his mark with a tragedy of 1732 called *Belisario*, and then turned to comedy, churning out no fewer than 250 plays until his death in 1793.

Venetian theatre has not always been well received. 'The comedies that I saw at Venice, or indeed in any other part of Italy, are very indifferent, and more lewd than those of other countries,' Joseph Addison judged at the beginning of the eighteenth century. 'Their poets have no notion of genteel comedy, and fall into the most filthy double meanings imaginable, when they have a mind to make their audience merry.' He put this fault chiefly down to the fact that the plays featured, for the most part, only four stock characters: Doctor, Harlequin, Pantalone and Coviello.

Undeniably, British writers also contributed their fair share of smut to Venice. Thomas Coryate, who walked to the city from Odcombe in Somerset in 1608 (calculating the distance as 952 miles), described Venice as 'the most glorious, peerelesse and mayden Citie', but he also lauded its courtesans. Four centuries later Byron – though he once described upper-class Venetian women as 'ugly as Virtue herself' – enthusiastically endorsed Coryate's opinion. And, unlike Addison, Byron relished the Venetian burlesque tradition, studying it and basing his own *Beppo: a Venetian story* on what he had learned.

In Campo San Bartolomeo, Goldoni's statue turns its back on the street that leads to Venice's most celebrated bridge, the Ponte Rialto. This is the oldest surviving bridge spanning the Grand Canal, designed by Antonio da Ponte at the end of the sixteenth century. Its single, 48-metre-high arch carries three passages, with a couple of rows of shops on the outer ones. Byron adored the dusky shadows which chequer it at night, and so do I.

Shakespeare gave his merchant of Venice a shop on the Rialto bridge. Today the marketeers of the city still throng the neigh-bouring streets and markets (the *Fabbricche Vecchie*, comple-mented by the *Fabbricche Nuove*, which Sansovino designed in 1555). Outside the markets, the stalls surround and almost swamp the oldest church in Venice, San Giacomo, which a Greek founded in 421, though its present form dates from the eleventh century. Its inscription prays, 'May your cross, O Christ, be the salvation of this place. Around this temple may the law of the merchant be just, his weights fair and his contracts joyful.' Whether you get value for money from the wine, vegetables, leather goods, cheap trinkets and masks sold here now is anyone's guess.

Cross back over the Rialto bridge, turn right alongside the Grand Canal, walk past a portrait relief of nineteenth-century Italian patriot Giuseppe Mazzini, who carries a copy of his own book *Doveri Del Uomo* (*On the Duties of Man*) and, by way of two palaces, the narrow Calle Bembo and its continuation, the Calle Fabbri, you reach the heart of Venice, Piazza San Marco.

Its campanile, which anyone who arrives at Venice's main airport will already have glimpsed with a thrill, began life as a lighthouse and was raised to its present height in the sixteenth century. In 1452 it is said that the Emperor Frederick III Barbarossa rode to the top on horseback up a spiral ramp. Certainly Galileo later demonstrated his newly invented telescope to the doge from the summit of this campanile. It suddenly collapsed on 14 July 1902, and was rebuilt as an exact copy (strengthened, one hopes). At its base is the Loggetta, a meeting place designed by Jacopo Sansovino for Venetian patricians. He also designed the statues of Pallas Athenae, Mercury, Apollo and Peace over its three arches.

Pigeons either delight or irritate you in this square. Under awnings musicians play for customers rich enough to afford a coffee or an ice-cream in the open-air cafés. To the east rises the façade of San Marco, fronted by flagstaffs on bronze pedestals, designed by Alessandro Leopardi in 1505.

We owe the present aspect of the basilica of San Marco to architects commissioned by Doge Domenico Contarini, who ruled from 1043 to 1070. Domenico himself did not live to see the building, for its five cupolas were completed only in 1095. John Ruskin memorably described it as:

A treasure heap, it seems, partly of gold, and partly of opal and mother of pearl, hollowed beneath into five great vaulted porches, ceiled with fair mosaic, and beset with sculpture of alabaster, clear as amber and delicate as ivory – sculpture fantastic and involved of palm leaves and lilies, and grapes and pomegranates, and birds clinging and fluttering among the branches, all twined together into an endless network of buds and plumes; and in the midst of it, the solemn forms of angels, sceptred, and robed to the feet, and leaning to each other across the gates, their figures indistinct among the gleaming of the golden ground through the leaves beside them, interrupted and dim, like the morning light as it faded back among the branches of Eden, when first its gates were angel-guarded long ago.

In truth, the basilica is guarded by bronze copies of four noble Roman horses, brought here from Constantinople at the beginning of the fourteenth century.

The mosaic on the façade depicting the translation of the relics of St Mark to Venice dates from the twelfth century, while the rest were added in the eighteenth. In the form of a Greek cross, modelled on the church of the Holy Apostles in Constantinople (which is no more), the interior of the basilica is covered with over 5,000 square metres of mosaics. Doge Domenico Salvi (whose wife was Greek) commissioned Greek mosaicists from Torcello to create them. Other mosaicists came from Ravenna, long an outpost of Byzantine culture. Later artists added Gothic elements to the whole, yet the overall ensemble remains a stupendous example of the Byzantine style.

Inside I think that the finest mosaics are those from the thirteenth and fourteenth centuries, notwithstanding the fact that men of the calibre of Titian, Tintoretto and Veronese made drawings for later ones. From the thirteenth century comes the mosaic of the Passion, which is flanked by those depicting Pentecost and Christ's ascension. The glamorous Gothic mosaics in the baptistry (depicting the life of St John the Baptist, the events surrounding the birth of Jesus, and the crucifixion) were commissioned in the mid-fourteenth century by the humanist Doge Andrea Dandolo, who is buried there. In the scene where Salome appears bearing the severed head of John the Baptist, King Herod is dressed as a Byzantine emperor.

The oldest mosaics in the basilica, dating perhaps from the late eleventh century or from the early twelfth, cover the choir, which is separated from the rest of the building by a Gothic iconostasis, designed in 1394 by Jacobello and Pietro Paolo dalle Massegne and bearing statues of the Blessed Virgin, St John the Evangelist and the twelve apostles, with the crucified Jesus. The four angels of the Apocalypse above it date from the thirteenth century.

St Mark's square is enlivened by a clock tower, designed at the end of the fifteenth century by Mauro Coducci, with two bronze Moors striking the hours by hammering a huge bell; as well as by Coducci's Procuratie Vecchie on the north side, whose arches are matched by those of the Procuratie Nuove, built by Baldassare Longhena and Vincenzo Scamozzi on the south side. The square is closed off by the Fabbrica Nuova, which Napoleon Bonaparte commissioned in 1810.

And at the far end of a little piazza to the left of the basilica of San Marco is the chunky Bridge of Sighs, built by Antonio Contino in order to bring prisoners for examination before the city's inquisitors. Byron sums up its spell in the opening couplet of *Childe Harold's Pilgrimage*:

> I stood in Venice, on the Bridge of Sighs,
> A palace and a prison on each hand.

Save for millionaires, this is no place to eat. Venetian food grows more and more expensive, the nearer you get to St Mark's square. As the price rises, so the choice diminishes. Eat instead in little restaurants nearer the main railway station or, better still, in some of the secluded piazzas I am describing in this tour. Many menus offer *fegato alla veneziana*, a scrumptious dish consisting simply of thin slices of liver cooked on sweet fried onions. I relish liver, and in Venice also adore *fegato in tortiera*, in which the thin liver slices have been coated in breadcrumbs before being fried in butter. They are served sprinkled with lemon and sugar. *Risi e bisi* is another Venetian treat, consisting of rice with peas and chopped ham. Fish dishes abound in this sea-faring city, a particularly succulent one to my mind being *saor*, sardines and onions fried in oil. Finally, the Austrian occupation of Venice enriched the city's cuisine with goulash and lethally sweet cakes.

In the piazzetta to the right of San Marco stands the Doges' Palace, a Venetian Gothic masterpiece built for the rulers of Venice between 1309 and 1442. Pink marble from Verona and white marble from Istria clad a wall rising from arches and supporting six Gothic windows. Embellishing the façade are carvings, perhaps by Matteo Raverti, of drunken Noah, the archangel Gabriel, Adam and an almost naked Eve. Jacopo della Quercia (1374–1438) carved here a 'Judgement of Solomon', which is topped by Gabriel again, this time in avenging mood.

Inside is a staircase designed by Antonio Rizzo, adorned with massive statues of Neptune and Mars sculpted by Jacopo Sansovino. The massive main hall, where 1,700 Venetian patricians once debated, dates from 1340. Its entrance wall boasts the biggest oil painting in the world, twenty-two metres by ten, painted by Tintoretto. Said Tintoretto on receiving the commission, 'I thank the senators for according me paradise in this life, hoping that by the grace of God I shall also attain it in the next.' Ruskin sourly commented that Tintoretto did not paint it to make anyone think of heaven, but simply 'to form a beautiful termination for the hall of the Greater Council'.

For the great hall Veronese contributed another masterpiece: the ceiling fresco of 'The Triumph of Venice'. Here too is Domenico Tintoretto's frieze of seventy-six doges. One of them is blacked out: Marin Falier, put to death for treason in 1355. Falier's crime, according to his fellow-senators, was to have attempted to exalt the powers of the doge at their expense. The inscription found where once his portrait was reads, 'Hic est locus Marini Falethri decapitati pro criminibus' ('On this spot was once Marin Falier, beheaded because of his crimes'). It is pleasing to remember that Byron warmed to Falier and made him the subject of a five-act tragedy. This doge, Byron judged, 'appears to have been a man of talent and courage', adding that Falier also seemed 'to have been of an ungovernable temper'. Byron's tragedy ends with Falier's execution, the populace rushing towards the great staircase of the Doges' Palace and one of them exclaiming, 'The gory head rolls down the Giants' Steps!'

A fire in 1574 meant that Andrea Palladio, among others, was commissioned to rebuild part of this palace. To him is due the Antepregadi, or 'room with four doors', with its stuccoed walls and paintings by Titian, Tintoretto and Tiepolo (who contributed the finest of these, 'Venice receiving the gifts of Neptune'). Palladio also designed the next room, the Sala del Collegio, with a lovely ceiling by Fra Bello and paintings by Veronese.

On the opposite side of the piazzetta from the Doges' Palace stands the very first example of Renaissance architecture in Venice, the Old Library, which Jacopo Sansovino designed in the mid-sixteenth century. If you walk across the piazzetta to the quayside and turn right, you can stroll beside the water towards the start of the Grand Canal.

Still in the Piazzetta di San Marco, atop a red granite column set up here in 1177 growls an extraordinary winged beast, cast in bronze. Commonly known as the lion of Venice, it is nothing of the kind. Early Christian art soon adopted the winged lion of the Book of Revelation as the symbol of St Mark the Evangelist. When, as legend has it, Mark himself, travelling from Aquileia to Rome, came ashore at Venice and an angel announced to him, 'Your body shall rest here', it was inevitable that his symbol should become that of La Serenissima.

The atmosphere of Venice is not caring of its masterpieces, and in 1892 the creature was discovered to be in need of restoration. Prompted by this, scholars, who had previously taken it to be a medieval statue, discovered a decree of 1293 declaring not only that the so-called lion was in place then but that even at that time it needed looking after by restorers. So, these earlier scholars wrongly concluded, the lion must have arrived in Venice as part of the booty brought here after the sack of Constantinople in 1204. They ignored the fact that the four horses that arrived here then are mentioned in contemporary chronicles, while the lion is not.

For this is no Christian beast. In 1985 the creature was once again taken from its column for restoration and, virtually for the first time, archaeologists and art historians could properly examine it. Their general conclusion was that, underlying the many later additions to the bronze, the so-called lion of St Mark was initially created in the Near East for a pagan cult (or maybe as a funeral monument) around 300 BC. Some people conjecture that the symbol of Mark the Evangelist may well once have had horns.

The penultimate time that the statue left Venice was in 1797, stolen by the French. In 1815, as the French were about to return him to Italy, workmen dropped the beast, smashing him into twenty pieces, and the weird, noble animal had to be restored (apparently for the fourth time in its long life) the following year, after its return to its customary home.

In October 1990 the creature visited Britain, to be displayed until 13 January 1991 in the foyer of the British Museum. While the beast was in London, I paused to admire him two or three times a week as I hurried into the British Library. As I walked around his face, he seemed to me to change from a cat to a Pekinese dog, from an ape to a griffin. As I left for a little lunchtime refreshment in one of the nearby taverns (or with my publishers at Aurum Press, who live close by in Museum Street), his creamy-white eyes followed me, and I wondered whether he might leap down from his pedestal and come along. The following autumn as I stared up at him, back in Venice, I am certain that as he remembered our meetings in London one of those eyes (the right one) winked at me.

The twin column in this square carries the statue of St Theodore, the first patron saint of the city, whom Mark supplanted. Beside him is his dragon, perhaps a pet, perhaps an adversary (for nothing properly historical is known about this fourth-century martyr).

On the opposite side of the lagoon rise two churches, both domed, both with classical, white marble façades. Both can be visited by taking water bus no. 5 from here. The nearer church, San Giorgio Maggiore, stands on the Isola di San Giorgio Maggiore and boasts a campanile as attractive as that in St Mark's square. Its artistic treasures include Carpaccio's 'St George and the Dragon', Titian's 'Last Supper' and 'The Fall of Man', a 'Coronation of the Virgin' by Tintoretto and Jacopo Bassano's 'Adoration of the Shepherds'. Forty-eight stalls, dating from the 1590s, were sculpted by the Belgian A. van den Brulle. And the church preserves the papal tiara of Pius VII, who was elected in 1800 by a conclave sitting here. Beside the church are two cloisters, one built in the fifteenth century by Andrea Buora, the other begun by Palladio and finished by Baldassare Longhena.

The second church across the lagoon is the Redentore, the work of Palladio, which rises on the Isola della Giudecca. Conceived by Doge Alvise Mocenigo as a thank-offering from those who had survived the savage plague of 1577 (one of whose victims was Titian), it was to be dedicated to Jesus Christ, the Saviour. The site was perfect for Palladio, whose architectural palate included the notion of buildings seen from afar, on which the play of light and shade would entrance the viewer. As well as displaying his refined adaptation of classical Roman forms, the architecture of the Redentore possessed a theological significance, as part of a project conceived by the Council of Trent, in which Christians tempted to align themselves with the dangerous theories of the

Reformation would be beguiled back to Catholicism by the aesthetic beauty of new churches. In addition, these churches were to be designed in a fashion that would allow every worshipper to participate fully in the Mass and to hear the word of God.

Accordingly, Palladio first designed his church as a complete circle, the altar at the centre beneath an imposing dome of the sort already exploited by Bramante and Michelangelo in Rome. His view was considered too revolutionary, and he was forced to modify the plan; yet he still contrived to build a church whose central space is austerely grand.

Also across the water from the quayside of the piazzetta rise the double domes and golden globe of the church of Santa Maria della Salute. Like the Redentore, this church was built as a thank-offering after Venice had survived another plague, this one in 1630. Its architect was Baldassare Longhena, and he designed it in the shape of a crown, to signify the heavenly coronation of the Blessed Virgin Mary. Santa Maria della Salute was finished only in 1687, five years after Longhena's death. Its powerful baroque interior contains some superb works of art, notably (in the sacristy) Titian's 'Cain and Abel', his 'Sacrifice of Abraham' and his 'David and Goliath'. These were painted in his maturity, but the church also contains a painting of 'St Mark surrounded by saints' done when Titian was in his twenties. Here too is a 1551 painting of 'The Marriage of Cana' by Tintoretto. The imposing high altar is by Longhena himself.

From here you can easily walk to the Palazzo Venier dei Leoni, which was begun in 1749 by Lorenzo Boschetti and never finished. In consequence the Venetians dub it the *non finito*. For thirty years, until her death in 1979, the American art collector Peggy Guggenheim lived here, and today the palace houses the treasures of modern art that she amassed, including works by her husband Max Ernst.

To take a water bus from the Piazza San Marco back along the Grand Canal to the church of the Scalzi is one of the treats of Venice. On either side rise gilded and decorated palaces, painted with the rich reds discovered by the great Venetian artists. The colours of this city entranced Ruskin:

While the burghers and barons of the North were building their dark streets and grisly castles of oak and sandstone, the merchants of Venice were covering their palaces with porphyry and gold; and at last, when her mighty painters had created for her a colour more priceless than gold or porphyry, even this, the richest of the treasures, she lavished upon walls whose foundations were beaten by the sea: and the strong tide, as it runs beneath the Rialto, is reddened to this day by the frescos of Giorgione.

Alight first at the wooden Academy bridge (constructed in the 1930s to replace its faulty nineteenth-century predecessor) for a visit to the Accademia art gallery. Its masterpieces include one of Mantegna's rare surviving works, a portrait of a lissome St George, as well as works by almost every other great Venetian painter. If one regrets that the lower left-hand corner of Vittore Carpaccio's 'Miracle of the Relic of the Cross at the Rialto Bridge' was sliced off in the mid-sixteenth century, so that a new doorway could be cut in the gallery, can one take comfort from the fact that no less a genius than Titian was consulted before the atrocity was perpetrated? If one regrets that the gallery contains more Venetian masterpieces than anyone could enjoy in a lifetime, may I urge you to return to Mantegna's 'St George'? As we shall see at Padua, there one of Mantegna's greatest masterpieces has been miserably destroyed (see p.114). Here the artist leaps to life again. The saint's staff pierces the frame of the painting; a burnished bronze halo reflects the back of his head, a brilliantly innovative use of that conventional sign of a saint; a green dragon lies vanquished at his feet; and a dusty Italian road curves seductively up to a hill town behind him.

Emerging from the gallery, pause on the Academy bridge to look back along the canal at Santa Maria della Salute. Close by the bridge, on the right bank of the Grand Canal, is the complex Palazzo Mocenigo, once the home of Byron. For him those were idyllic days. 'I have the Palazzo Mocenigo on the Canal' Grande for three years to come, and a pretty villa in the Euganean hills for the Summer for nearly the same term,' he wrote to his publisher, John Murray, in 1818. 'While I remain in the city itself, I keep my horses on an island with a good beach, about half a mile from the town, so that I get a gallop of some miles along the shore of the Adriatic daily.'

Byron was writing *Don Juan*, whose verve and wit are undoubted, though few recommended it for family reading in the nineteenth century. A year later he was lamenting to Murray that he 'had written about a hundred stanzas of a *third* canto to *Don Juan*, but the reception of the first two is not encouragement to you nor me to proceed'.

From the Academy bridge take water bus no. 1 for two stops to San Tomà, to make your way across the peaceful Campo San Tomà, with its Renaissance well and church with a Corinthian façade, into Campo dei Frari. Franciscan monks created the superb, high brick Gothic church of the Frari, their second one on this spot, beginning in the 1330s and completing the building a century or so later. Spare marble enhances its stark façade. Above its entrance is a statue of the risen Jesus, sculpted by Alessandro Vittoria in 1581. On two other columns are statues of the Virgin Mary and St Francis, which were sculpted by Bartolommeo Buon a century earlier.

The interior is simple, but the tombs decidedly not so. The most astounding is that of Doge Giovanni Pesaro, which is supported by four straining negroes in tattered clothing, along with two grisly skeletons holding inscriptions. Another strange tomb is a pyramid monument, designed by Antonio Canova in 1794, into whose dread darkness walk melancholy mourners. Over the high altar hangs Titian's 'Assumption', painted when he was forty-one years hold. St Peter kneels before the scene; St Thomas points in wonder. The painting is signed: Ticianus.

The chapter house of the Frari houses late fifteenth-century works by Alvise and Bartolomeo Vivarini, and a triptych by

Titian's master, Giovanni Bellini (this painting signed Johannes Bellinus); but it is worth visiting simply to see a painting of 1339, the 'Virgin Mary' of Paolo Veneziano. Only with Maestro Paolo, who died in 1362, does Venetian painting – while still displaying its Byzantine origins – truly emanicipate itself. With him, his pupils and his two sons a new intimacy entered Venetian art.

Cross the Ponte dei Frari opposite the west door of the church, turn right, then left into Rio Terra and second right, to cross over another canal into Campo di San Paolo. Here is another peaceful square, neglected by the crowds who pack Venice. Its intimate jettied houses adjoin fine palaces: the fifteenth-century Gothic Palazzo Soranzo; the sixteenth-century Palazzo Corner Mocenigo; and the eighteenth-century Palazzo Tiepolo-Maffetti. As for the church of this *campo*, San Paolo has a fourteenth-century campanile and a fifteenth-century doorway. Inside are paintings by Giandomenico Tiepolo (the son of Giambattista), the finest being his 'Way of the Cross'. Here too is a 'Last Supper' by Tintoretto, Veronese's 'Marriage of the Virgin Mary' and Giambattista Tiepolo's 'The Virgin appearing to St John Nepomuk'.

Walk back to Campo dei Frari and now turn left across the bridge opposite the west door. Crossing another bridge, follow Calle della Chiesa into a little piazza, turning left and then right at the far side. Hidden away in this street is the Scuola Grande di San Giovanni Evangelista, its courtyard faced by a splendid marble screen, which Pietro Lombardo designed in 1481.

From here you can return to the main railway station of Venice by means of a leisurely five-minute walk, taking you by way of the canal Rio Marin. Gondolas are romantic but extremely expensive; gondoliers have long had an evil reputation. Even in the early seventeenth century, Thomas Coryate dubbed gondoliers 'the most vicious and licentious varlets in all the city'. My own view is that the best way of enjoying gondolas after dusk is to lean over the bridge across the Rio Marin. Packs of them pass underneath, with a little light flickering at each end, an accordion playing in one, a singer in another.

Many consider this music kitsch. But even Richard Wagner (who died in Venice on 13 February 1883, in the Renaissance Palazzo Vendramin-Calergi on the Grand Canal) confessed that the gondoliers' plaintive songs might have inspired the opening of the third act of his *Tristan*. As for Byron, he spotted the erotic possibilities of the quaint barge and its music:

> They wait in their dusk livery of woe,
> But not to them do woeful things belong,
> For sometimes they contain a deal of fun,
> Like mourning coaches when the funeral's done.

Henry James, who adored the city of Venice, found it enraptured him best of all from a gondola. 'I simply see a narrow canal in the heart of the city,' he recalled, 'a patch of green water and a surface of pink wall. The gondola moves slowly; it gives a great smooth swerve, passes under a bridge, and the gondolier's cry, carried over the quiet water, makes a kind of splash in the stillness.'

Venetan villas and the
city of Palladio

Though much copied, the Venetan villa is unique. Some 300,000 of them dot the Veneto, built from the early fifteenth to the nineteenth centuries. Sometimes they cluster together; sometimes a single one dominates some far-flung region. Their architecture is invariably entrancing, yet also astonishingly varied. Their existence springs from powerful historical and economic factors, and even those which, at present, are in a pitiful state of repair (despite the heroic efforts of two determined conservation bodies, the Ente per le Ville Venete, which was set up in 1958, and the Instituto Regionale per le Ville Venete, which replaced it in 1978) speak, by their very condition, of Italy's social history.

As we have seen, the fortunes of Venice took a decisive turn in the early fifteenth century, when her dominant trading position with the east was suddenly reversed. In consequence the city fathers, the princes, the nobles and unpretentious farmers sought to develop a new economy in the hinterland of the city. Over the next 200 years much of their capital was increasingly devoted to agricultural land, and above all to the cultivation of maize. Land was reclaimed; the potential fertility of the Po valley was exploited. In the fifteenth-century equivalents of the modern provinces of Vicenza, Verona, Treviso and Padua, the marshes were drained and hitherto fallow fields ploughed. Meadows were irrigated and planted with rice. Vineyards and orchards were established. Flocks of sheep grazed. Silkworms fed on mulberry trees.

This development was eased by peace. Medieval Veneto had been the scene of continual conflicts, sometimes between great families, such as the Scaligers, the Visconti and the Carraresi, as Venice attempted to spread her rule west. The last major attack on her expansion was led by the violent Pope Julius II, who, having vainly urged La Serenissima to relinquish that part of Romagna that she had occupied in 1503, allied with France and Germany forcibly to win them back. Six years later he excommunicated Venice and, as a member of the League of Cambrai (which also included France, Spain and Germany), wrested from her Rimini and Faenza, usurping her right to taxes from these territories. Happily at this point the Pope, needing an ally against possible Turkish invasion, decided that he had weakened Venice enough and made peace.

It now became possible for the industrious to establish themselves as large landowners in the Venetian hinterland. Twice a year, in spring and autumn, the landowner needed to put in an appearance to supervise his underlings as they sowed the crops, reaped the harvest, tended his beasts, gathered the grapes and annually cut wood for winter and for building. Accordingly, these landowners built for themselves country houses, some of them initially quite modest.

Inevitably in such a productive era, craftsmen flourished. Medieval skills re-emerged in a secular environment. Plasterers embellished the new villas with stucco-work; painters frescoed the walls, inside and out; smiths wrought iron gateways and verandahs; gardeners pushed their domains beyond the walls of medieval defences to create virtual parks around the villas; and, above all, a new breed of architect blossomed.

The earliest of these villas were, of course, Gothic in style. Here are some to look out for. At Carmignano di Brenta in the province of Padua (some thirty-six kilometres north-west of Padua itself), Villa Spessa is a flamboyant Gothic country house built in the mid-fifteenth century by Giovanni da Quinto and retaining some of its external frescos, their faded yellows, reds and greens framing ogival windows. (You have to telephone in advance for a visit – 049-5957313.) At Negrar in the province of Verona (and around seven kilometres north-west of Verona itself) stands the late sixteenth-century Villa Veritá Serego Alighieri (which you can visit in summer on Tuesdays and Thursdays from 16.00 to 18.00 and in winter on Thursday mornings from 10.30 to 12.30).

Of the Gothic villas in the province of Vicenza, which are by far the most numerous, the mid-sixteenth-century Villa Saraceno was based on a fourteenth-century house. It lies thirty kilometres south of Vicenza, and can be seen if you telephone in advance (0444-891084). Another Gothic country home, the fifteenth-century Villa Brendola, sixteen kilometres south-west of Vicenza, can be visited each morning from Monday to Saturday and also on Tuesday and Friday afternoons.

Gothic villas are comparatively rare in the Veneto, for Renaissance architecture soon made its mark on these country houses. Twelve kilometres south-west of Treviso you can, on any morning, visit a fine and simple one: Villa Caliari at Sasale sul Sile, built in the second half of the sixteenth century, with an early seventeenth-century façade. At Volargne di Dolcè, twenty-two kilometres north-west of Verona, Renaissance architects such as Michele Sanmicheli helped to transform a fifteenth-century villa into a Renaissance home (open to the public mornings and afternoons, except on Mondays, and frescoed in the eighteenth century with sybils and scenes from the Apocalypse).

As many landowners came to discover the delights of the Venetan countryside, some of them became reluctant to quit it for the city. As a result, their villas grew more and more magnificent, in part also because maize proved an extremely profitable crop. Laudably, these landlords seem to have had no desire to separate themselves too firmly from their workforce. Instead, one of the major developments in the architecture of their villas integrated in one unit every member of these rustic communities – farmhands and their families, dovecotes, stables and byres, barns in which the hay and corn were stored and of course, at the centre of the whole complex, the sumptuous home of the landowner himself.

One genius transformed this functional scheme into masterpiece after masterpiece. Andrea di Pietro della Gondola, whom we know as Palladio, was born in 1508 and died in 1580. Apprenticed to a Paduan stone-carver at the age of thirteen, he so chafed at his restricted life that in 1524 he broke his contract and escaped to Vicenza. The city was already endowed with lovely houses, palaces and villas. Palladio was to outbuild them all. Many of the buildings left unfinished after his death in 1580 were completed by his exceedingly talented disciple Scamozzi, who had another thirty-seven years to live.

Imitated probably more than any other architect of his era, Palladio had the knack – or rather the genius – of taking over ancient Roman forms and making them entirely his own. He was a man, as Goethe avowed, 'so strongly imbued with the instincts of the ancients that he acutely felt the petty, narrow spirit of his own times and, instead of conforming to it, set about transforming it'. The sunshine of the Veneto, and the white stones, stucco and marbles available to him, enabled him also to experiment brilliantly with the play of light and shade. The fact that his patrons tended to commission brick and stucco buildings, rather than stone and marble, means that some of these acknowledged masterpieces have deteriorated alarmingly over the centuries. Others have been superbly restored.

As a humanist, Palladio turned to antiquity seeking inspiration for his innovative buildings, which were to influence European domestic architecture for the following three centuries. He studied classical monuments and wrote two guidebooks to Roman antiquities. Palladio warmed to his predecessor Vitruvius, the first-century AD Roman military engineer who wrote the sole treatise on architecture to have survived from the ancient world. Twenty-two years before Palladio's birth, the first printed edition of Vitruvius's seminal work had been published.

Palladio also responded to the genius of the brilliant Renaissance architect Leon Battista Alberti, who had built the churches of San Francesco at Rimini and Santa Maria Novella at Florence and, in 1485, had published a ten-volume study of antique Roman architecture. The Venetan genius likewise relished the work of Michelangelo. And in 1570 he published his own *I Quattro libri dell'architettura (The Four Books of Architecture)*, setting out the principles that had guided his own buildings. Illustrating his theses with detailed, cleanly drawn woodcuts, Palladio devoted a major part of his work to his own principle achievement, the creation of country houses.

If this sounds dry-as-dust, Andrea Palladio's Venetan villas are decidedly not. As you come upon them (and you will repeatedly do so in this book), their diversity and their virtuosity are startling. The older pattern of the Venetan villa either had towers at both sides of a horizontal block, consisting of a portico below and a loggia above, or else consisted of a single block, which dispensed with towers and boasted mullioned windows.

Palladio's villas, by contrast, frequently included a palatial residence for the landowner, from which spread long porticoes (known as *barchese*) linking his home with the outbuildings in which lived the workers, horses and cattle. The master of a household, Palladio insisted, must:

be able to go to every place under cover, that neither the rains, nor the scorching sun of the summer, may be a nuisance to him, when he goes to look after his affairs; which will also be of great use to lay wood under cover, and an infinite number of things belonging to a villa, that would otherwise be spoiled by the rains and the sun; besides which these porticoes will be a great ornament.

41

Despite his infinite variety, one feels at home with Palladio, for in the eighteenth century British architects such as William Kent and Robert Adam adored and imitated him. In 1786 Goethe, desperately seeking in Verona a copy of Palladio's *I Quattro libri dell'architettura*, eventually found not an original edition but a facsimile published by the former English consul in Venice. 'The English should be given credit for having appreciated so long what is good,' Goethe noted, 'and for their munificence and wonderful skill in publicizing it.'

The first English translation of Palladio's *I Quattro libri dell'architettura* was in fact an inadequate one, made by the Venetian architect Gioacomo Leoni in 1715. Even some of Palladio's original engravings were altered, in line with contemporary baroque taste. Then the architect and patron of artists, Richard Boyle, third Earl of Burlington, inspired an exact translation (by Isaac Ware) and accurate reproductions, which was published in 1738. I think this must be the work that Goethe bought, and it is this translation that I use here.

As a countryman, Palladio insisted that the working animals, and especially their dunghills, should be situated at a proper distance from the master's habitation. As a careful organizer of his clients' interests, he designed complex villas where the stewards and bailiffs were housed near the gates, to deter intruders. As a man born poor, he suggested that wine cellars 'must be made somewhat sloping in the middle, and have their floors of terrazzo, or paved in such a manner, that should the wine happen to run out, it may be taken up again'. Finally, as a working architect, he was cunning enough to flatter his patrons and thus acquire more. As he noted, for example, at the end of his description of Count Giacomo Angarano's villa, at Angarano in the province of Vicenza, 'This place is celebrated for the good wines that are more there, and the fruits that grow there, but much more for the courtesy of the master.'

He also had inspired opinions concerning how best to utilize the lie of the land.

When there is a necessity of building upon a mountain, let a situation be chosen facing a temperate part of the heaven, and which is not by higher mountains continually shaded, nor scorched (as it were by two suns) by the sun's reverberation from some neighbouring rock.

He deplored building villas in valleys, where the humidity infects both the body and the mind, and through which winds blow with fury. Hay-lofts, he insisted, must look south or west, 'because the hay being dried by the heat of the sun, it will not be in danger of corrupting and taking fire'. Granaries, by contrast, ought to open to the north, 'because the corn cannot so easily be heated, but rather cooled by the winds; and thereby it will be a long time preserv'd, and none of those little animals will breed there, which damage it very much'. All this you see again and again in the Veneto, in the villas he built and in those of his disciples.

Palladio liked to enhance the status of the main residence by raising it on a stepped base and giving it a temple-like pediment. Porches were one of his specialities, especially as Vitruvius had identified five different kinds. On each side, he suggested, 'small halls might be made, that would look over the gardens'.

Landowners were growing richer, and the interiors of Palladian villas reveal this. Frescos sometimes covered every wall; sculptures enhanced niches and gardens. In 1560 artists of the calibre of Paolo Veronese were decorating such sumptuous homes as Villa Barbaro at Maser, which we shall later visit (see p.146). Palladio built it from 1560 for Daniele de Barbaro, patriarch of Aquileia, and his brother Marcantonio. Again this exquisite villa has a central block, raised on steps, with an escutcheoned pediment, joined by porticoes to two side buildings, while the garden is enhanced with statuary. Villa Barbaro also boasts a lily pool, shaded by a pedimented building in golden stone, with sculptures by Marcantonio Barbaro himself.

Villa Emo Capodilista, at Fanzolo di Vedelago (some twenty-three kilometres west of Treviso), is another Palladian villa, again with a rich pediment which, like that of Villa Barbaro, rises on

Doric pillars. Once again porticoes stretch to each wing, and there are statues in the garden. But the effect of this villa, built for the Venetian patrician Leonardo Emo between 1561 and 1566, is quite different: sterner, less fanciful, cooler. (Only inside does it become suddenly sumptuous, under the rich decorative hand of G. B. Zelotti, whose *trompe-l'oeil* characters seem to be ready to tumble out of the wall; see also pp.142–3.)

By contrast, at Poiana Maggiore, forty-two kilometres south of Vicenza, Villa Poiana is a simple, geometrical block, its pediment unadorned save for three statues, its interior frescoed by Bernardino India and Andelmo Canello. (The villa is open daily, mornings and afternoons.)

Yet Palladio's undoubted pre-eminence should not obscure the fact that other superb contemporary architects also created Venetan villas. At Polesella, fourteen kilometres south-west of Rovigo, you can visit (if you phone there first, 049-701482) Villa Morosini Mantovani, named after Francesco Morosini, who was doge of Venice from 1688 to 1694, but built a century earlier by Vincenzo Scamozzi and frescoed under his supervision. In 1576 Scamozzi also designed the impressive, square and spare Villa Pisani at Lonigo, known as 'La Rocca' (twenty-five kilometres south-west of Vicenza), with its circular salon, hexagonal dome and Doric portico. (Telephone 0444-830364 to arrange a visit.)

Another architectural genius of the sixteenth century, the Florentine Jacopo Sansovino, built Villa Garzoni Carraretto at Pontecasale di Candiana, south-east of Padua, in 1536. Telephone in advance (049-5349602) to explore Sansovino's superb colonnaded courtyard, with a well also designed by him, and the villa's late eighteenth-century decorations by Francesco Gallimberti.

The Veneto fell on evil times in the early seventeenth century. Plagues ravaged most of Europe; sporadic warfare dogged the region; and the Turks menaced from the east. But as conditions improved, villas – some of them imposing – again proliferated. In 1666, for instance, Antonio Pizzocaro built the grandiose

Villa Piovene (also known as Villa da Schio) with its porticoed courtyard at Castelgomberto, twenty-five kilometres north-west of Vicenza.

To be given a guided tour of another magnificent late-seventeenth century villa, telephone Villa Pesara at Este, thirty-one kilometres south-west of Padua (0429-2101). Designed by Baldassare Longhena around 1670, it was frescoed by a follower of Tiepolo, Giovanni Scagliaro, between 1760 and 1790. To Longhena we also owe the splendid mid-seventeenth-century Villa Widman Borletti at Bagnoli di Sopra, situated fifteen or so kilometres north-east of Rovigo, whose church, theatre and gardens, with statues by Adriano Bonazza, you can visit on Thursday afternoons.

Giorgio Massari flourished in the next century. His finest villa, I think, is Villa Cordellina Lombardi at Montecchio Maggiore, twelve kilometres south-west of Vicenza, built between 1735 and 1760 for his fellow Venetian Carlo Cordellina Molin. Its double-storeyed central hall was ravishingly frescoed in 1743 by yet another Venetian, Giambattista Tiepolo, to whom we also owe the statues in the garden. (This villa is open from 4 to 28 April and from 5 May to 18 July on Wednesdays and at weekends.)

Venetan nobles continued to build villas with *brio*. One curiosity is Villa Tacoli Dionisi at Cerea (which lies thirty-four kilometres south-east of Verona, and is open from May to September on Wednesday afternoons). Its first owner, the Marchese Gabriele. Dionisi, was a retired soldier and also its architect, and its interior decorations are devoted to his own glorification.

Yet because the lords and the workers lived in such close proximity, a fresco by even the most eminent painter might still depict a rustic scene. Villa Valmarana at Vicenza ('which you can visit daily, except on Mondays, from 5 March to 5 November) was built by Giovan Maria Bertoldo in the late 1660s. In 1757 Giambattista Tiepolo, his son Giandomenico and Girolamo Mengozzi Colonna painted the interior. Some scenes have literary themes, representing the *Iliad*, the *Aeneid* and *Orlando Furioso*; but Giandomenico Tiepolo has also left us a fresco of a peasant family at lunch. They are eating out of doors, the father holding his naked baby on his knee, his pregnant wife standing as she feeds herself, an elder boy sitting on the ground and raising his soup bowl to his lips.

But these were suddenly dangerous times for such sumptuous homes. Between the fall of the Venetian republic and the establishment of the kingdom of Italy, agrarian hardship peaked. Next, forests were thoughtlessly cut down. And those who had felt oppressed by the landowning classes now took revenge on their lavish villas. Palladio had, after all, adapted the buildings of Roman antiquity for the governing classes of his time, and in subsequent eras their coats of arms continued to dominate the pediments of their country homes. Innocent symbols of oppression, these noble houses were now converted into barns, or simply allowed to fall into neglect. In the twentieth century some of them fared even worse, splendid villas being utilized in wartime as hospitals, military headquarters and munitions depots. A priceless patrimony of the Veneto was put at risk; and to some extent, even today, it remains at risk, with buildings still dilapidated, even though their original glory peers through the broken stone and flaking stucco.

The Romans established themselves at Vicenza at a settlement initially inhabited by the Ligurians. The Romans called the place Vicetia, and a few Roman remains still exist. So do parts of the city's medieval walls, nowadays vine-clad.

You can see some of the Roman remains to the west, just outside Vicenza, in the basilica of Santi Felice e Fortunato. This Romanesque church was founded in the fourth century, though its present form dates from the late tenth and twelfth centuries. Its campanile of 1166 seems more like a defensive keep than a belfry. Inside, among the remains of the first church, are the fourth-century crypt and a mosaic, in part from the

Constantine era, in part from that of Emperor Thodosius, who ruled in the late fourth century. The Lobia aqueduct, north of the city, was constructed by the Romans, and they also laid out the chequerboard pattern of the city streets – the Roman *Cardus* and *Decumanus* today revealed in the Corso Palladio, Contradà Porti and Contrà del Monte.

The barbarians ravaged the city and Attila the Hun virtually destroyed it. Slowly she rose again, however, under the rule of imperial bishops, who so oppressed the citizens that in 1164 they rebelled and set up a free municipality. Successively ruled by the Scaligers and the Visconti, from 1405 Vicenza came under the sway of the Venetians. Under their beneficence the city began to flourish, reaching its artistic apogee in the sixteenth century. A century later Joseph Addison judged that:

This sweete Towne has more well-built Palaces than any of its dimensions in all Italy, besides a number begun and not yet finished (but of stately designe) by reason of the domestic dissensions i'twixt them and those of Brescia, fomented by the sage Venetians lest by combining they might think of recovering their ancient liberty.

If you arrive in Vicenza by train, walk up Viale Roma and turn right through the remnants of the city walls and past Vicenza's medieval citadel. Instantly you reach three massive columns, designed by Palladio himself (or, some say, by his most gifted pupil, Vincenzo Scamozzi). Columns entranced Palladio's mathematical mind. He loved to analyse and brood on their proportions. He counselled that:

If a column be fifteen foot high, the thickness at the bottom must be divided into six parts and a half, five and a half of which will be the thickness for the top. If from fifteen to twenty foot high, divide the diameter at the bottom into seven parts, and six and a half will be the diameter above.

North of this piazza are laid out the Salvi gardens, watered by a canal and surrounding the Palladian Loggia Valmarana of 1592, a playful building with a noble flight of steps leading up to its entrance.

Returning to Palladio's columns, turn right into Piazza del Castello. To the right of the brick Porta Castello stands Palazzo Piovini, built in 1658 by Antonio Pizzocaro. Here is a fiery statue of Giuseppe Garibaldi. Rising at an angle to the piazza is Palazzo Porto-Breganze, built under Scamozzi's direction at the end of the sixteenth century, though designed by his master Palladio. Three elegant columns decorate its façade, a reminder that façades also fascinated Palladio, whose *Four Books of Architecture* contain exquisite engravings of several, as well as careful analyses of their forms.

Goethe, an architect himself, considered that Palladio's chief problem was how to make a proper use of columns in town houses and palaces, since the combination of columns and walls was an architectural contradiction. 'How industriously he worked on the problem, and how the presence of what he created makes us forget that we are being hypnotized!' he exclaimed at Vicenza. 'There is a divinity about his genius, comparable to that of a great poet,' he concluded.

Walk from here downhill past Vicenza's cathedral, whose Gothic façade of 1467 (attributed to Domenico Veneziano) is decorated in marble with white and pink lozenges. The campanile is Romanesque, the apse (finished in 1508) Renaissance, while the huge Gothic nave and chapels house paintings by Francesco Maffei, Bartolomeo Montagna and Lorenzo Veneziano. In Piazza del Duomo stands the episcopal palace, whose courtyard has an elegant Renaissance loggia, rising on arcades and designed by Bernardino da Milano in 1494. Excavations under Palazzo Proti, on the south side of the piazza, have uncovered Roman remains known as the Criptoportico.

Walking east from the cathedral you shortly reach the Piazzetta Andrea Palladio, in which stands a statue of the architect (placed here in 1859), and beyond it the magnificent Piazza dei Signori.

Palladio relished piazzas almost as much as villas, and had much to say about them. In sea ports, they ought to be near the water, he prescribed, but inland they should be at the centre of a town, convenient for every citizen. In his view, piazzas were also works of art: 'All the edifices that are made round a piazza ought not to be (according to ALBERTI) higher than the third part of the breadth of the piazza, nor lower than the sixth.' Arches he recommended, as giving ornament to piazzas. So did porticoes, as broad as their columns were high. Finally, he declared, 'On the part facing the warmest region of the heaven, on one side of the piazza, the basilica must be made, that is, the place where justice is administered, whither a great part of the people and men of business resort.'

For Vicenza's Piazza dei Signori, Palladio himself designed the magnificent basilica. It was a difficult job. In the mid-fifteenth century Domenico Veneziano had built a Gothic hall here with lovely brick vaults, known as the Palazzo della Ragione. In 1549 Palladio began its transformation, wrapping the palace in a huge classical envelope. He gave it two colonnaded galleries, one Doric in style, the other Ionic, and a golden copper roof. The Doric columns rise to a frieze of skulls. Of the sculpted rows of faces that decorate its façade, the upper ones are clean-shaven, the lower ones bearded. Palladio knew that he had created a masterpiece.

I do not doubt but this fabrick may be compared with the antient edifices, and ranked among the most noble, and most beautiful fabricks, that have been made since the antient times; not only for its grandeur, and its ornaments, but also for the materials, which is all very hard live stone, and all the stones have been banded and joined together with the utmost diligence.

The interior, which you can visit except on Sunday afternoons and Mondays, is massive, its ceiling like the upturned keel of a ship. Today it houses not the councillors of Vicenza but exhibitions.

Beside it rises the slender brick Torre di Piazza, which in the Middle Ages belonged to the Bissari family and in later years became the property of the municipality, which in the fourteenth century installed on it the first mechanical public clock.

The Gran Caffé Garibaldi, on the corner of Piazza dei Signori, is an excellent spot from which to admire the basilica, though for the privilege it charges more for its coffee or beer than most other establishments in the city. This is perhaps the moment to speak of the food and wine of Vicenza. The city's prize delicacy is probably *baccalà alla Vicentina* (cod, Vicenza-style). The cod is beaten viciously with a wooden hammer, soaked for thirty-six hours, cut into strips that are sprinkled with cheese and then delicately fried in butter, olive oil, anchovies and onions, before being cooked over a slow fire and seasoned with pepper, parsley and milk. Blue trout (*trota*) is another delicacy of this well-watered city. *Prosciutto* here is even graded like wine, the finest known as *il prosciutto DOC Veneto Berico Euganeo*. The Vicenzan dialect appears on menus, which dub roast pork (known elsewhere as *arrosto di Maiale*) *rosto de mas-scio*. A fiercer dish is the head of a pig, served on cheese and perfumed with truffles (*testa di porcino su fundata di formaggio dell'altopiano profumata al tartufo*).

Regional DOC wines to accompany such treats include both reds and whites, save that some of the whites are really golden in colour. Among these is Breganze Bianco, whose sister red is Breganze Rosso, and whose family includes the stronger, deeper red Breganze Cabernet and Breganze Pinot Nero. I very much like a pale yellow wine from the same slopes, Breganze Pinot Grigio, while Breganze Pinot Bianco is a delicate white still strong enough to complement one's *minestrone*. As for another golden white wine of the region, the very scent of Breganze Vespaiole makes one's soul twitch.

Wines from Colli Bérici are, I have found, generally slightly less strong in alcohol content than those labelled Breganze, while the ones labelled Gambellara are usually stronger – in the case of the golden Santo di Gambellara, sometimes achieving an alcohol content greater than 14 per cent.

On the same side of the Piazza dei Signori as the Gran Caffé

Garibaldi rises the arcaded and stuccoed Loggia del Capitaniato. This was the home of the Venetian governor of Vicenza, and was begun by Palladio in 1571, though he never quite completed it. Its columns blush pink. On its right stretches the long sixteenth-century Palazzo del Monte di Pietà, very haphazard and incorporating the baroque façade of the church of San Vicenzo, which dates from 1617.

Two free-standing pillars rise at the far end of the piazza. One carries the lion of St Mark, placed here in 1473, the other a statue of Jesus. Beyond them lies Piazza della Biade, in which stands the fifteenth-century church of Santa Maria dei Servi. Its façade was added in the eighteenth century, the entrance is Renaissance, but the interior (with a retable by Bartolomeo Montagna on the first altar on the right) remains Gothic.

The arcades of the ground floor of Palladio's basilica house shops and banks and shelter the stalls of booksellers. Beyond, you descend to the Piazza delle Erbe, where on Mondays, Tuesdays and Thursdays you will find a fruit and vegetable market. Here rises a medieval tower, linked to the basilica by an arch dating from 1494. Goethe, who adored Palladio's basilica, hated this medieval intrusion. 'Without doubt the architect's original plan was to demolish it,' he wrote, adding that he must control his anger because here, as elsewhere, he so frequently came upon what he loved and hated, side by side.

On this side of the city are a sprinkling of entertaining buildings. A little closer to the cathedral, in Via Pigafetta, rises a Gothic palace with a decidedly Spanish look, built in 1481. Here ten years later was born the navigator Antonio Pigafetta (hence the name of the building, Casa Pigafetta) who, between 1519 and 1522, sailed with Magellan around the world. The doorway bears the legend, 'No rose without a thorn', a reference to the Pigafetta coat of arms, which included three golden roses.

In nearby Contrà Piancoli rise (at no. 4) a Venetian Gothic building dating from the fifteenth century and (at no. 8) an early sixteenth-century house. Walk eastwards along Contrà San Paolo to cross the river by the singled arched Ponte San Michele of 1619, to find the oratory of San Nicola di Tolentino. He died in 1306 and was canonized by Pope Eugenius IV in 1446. His oratory at Vicenza was not begun until the next century and was finished in the eighteenth. The River Bacchiglione is one reason for Vicenza's former prosperity, being navigable from here to the Adriatic, pouring its waters into the sea at the ancient Portus Edronis, nowadays transformed into Chioggia.

On the other side of the city stands a superb collection of Renaissance and baroque buildings, most of them in Corso Andrea Palladio, and many of them designed by him. The *corso* runs eastwards from Piazza del Castello, passing the eighteenth-century church of the Filippini, whose façade of 1824 is by A. Piovene. Palazzo Bonin-Thiene at no. 13 is said to be the work of Palladio; the town hall (Palazzo del Commune) was begun in 1592 by Scamozzi and stuccoed inside in the eighteenth century; no. 57 is the late fifteenth-century Palazzo Braschi; and no. 45 is the fifteenth- and sixteenth-century Palazzo Capra (nowadays a bank).

After Palazzo Capra, the next street on the left is the Contradà Porti, whose palaces are superb. On the right the Palazzo Cavalloni-Thiene at no. 8 is a fifteenth-century Venetian Gothic building. In 1570 Palladio built no. 11, Palazzo Porto-Barbarano, with its massive façade. Opposite, the terracotta doorway and courtyard of no. 12, the Renaissance Palazzo Thiene, were created by Lorenzo da Bologna in 1489, though it is claimed that the façade at the rear overlooking Contrà Zanello is the work of Palladio. Next come two Gothic palaces (nos 14 and 17), Palazzo Sperotti-Trissino and Palazzo Porto-Breganza of 1481 (which is Venetian Gothic, save for Lorenzo da Bologna's Renaissance doorway and its porticoed courtyard).

Across the street, a plaque proclaims that here Luigi da Porto, who wrote the tale of Romeo and Juliet, died in May 1529 aged only forty-three. Beyond, the Renaissance architecture of no. 16, Palazzo Porto-Fontana, contrasts with the late fourteenth-century

Gothic of no. 19, Palazzo Colleoni-Porto, whose double balconies could well serve as the venue of the most famous scene in Shakespeare's play. Finally, no. 21 is Palladio's unfinished Palazzo Iseppo da Porto, with a façade of 1552.

Shortly you reach the River Bacchiglione, where you turn right along a street named Giuseppe Apolloni and first right into Contrà Giacomo Zanelli. Here are still more Gothic palaces with delicious double balconies. Gothic Palazzo Fontana-Sesso Zen (no. 2) was built in the fourteenth and fifteenth centuries, its style contrasting with the crenellated, late fifteenth-century Renaissance Palazzo Negri de Salvi. On the left of this street is the baroque church of Santo Stefano, which shelters a Madonna and saints by Palma the Elder. Further on, on the right, rises the Palladian façade of Palazzo Thiene.

Corso San Gaetano Thiene takes you back to Corso Andrea Palladio. Nearly every fine building in this street has a plaque detailing its history, save for two on the right, between here and Contradà Porti. These are the eighteenth-century church of San Gaetano, with its Corinthian façade and gesticulating statues, and no. 147, Vicenza's answer to the Ca' d'Oro of Venice, the Palazzo da Schio. This late fourteenth- and early fifteenth-century palace, with its sweet chimneys, is a piquant blend of Venetian Gothic and Renaissance architecture. Gerolama da Toso decorated its façade with paintings on a base of gold in 1532. It houses a collection of local antiquities amassed by the Schio family, with pre-Roman and Roman plaques and inscriptions.

Further east along the arcaded *corso*, the campanile and church of Santa Corona rise on the left. Dominican monks began building Santa Corona in 1261, though its architecture was enriched by Palladio himself. Its name derives from a spine of the crown of thorns worn by Jesus on the cross (and brought here by St Louis, King of France), which is enshrined in a fourteenth-century silver reliquary. Palladio too lies entombed in this church. The marquetry of the choir stalls dates from the late fifteenth century, and the high altar from 1669. But the two finest works of art in

Santa Corona are Giovanni Bellini's painting of the baptism of Jesus, and an 'Adoration of the Magi' by Paolo Veronese.

The house of Palladio (nos 165–7 Corso Palladio), although built in his style, was probably not his actual home. Yet Goethe found it delightful, in part because – supposing it really were Palladio's home – the architect, instead of building himself a palace, had created 'the least pretentious house in the world, with merely two windows even though the expanse of the wide wall would readily have accommodated a third'.

In Piazza Matteoti at the end of the *corso* are two of Palladio's supreme buildings, though they are quite different in character. Palazzo Chiericati, which he built in 1551 for Count Valerio Chiericato, is one of his most grandiose buildings. Palladio himself described it in his usual practical and laconic fashion.

This fabrick has in the part below a loggia forwards that takes in the whole front: the pavement of the first order rises above ground five foot; which has been done not only to put the cellars and other places underneath, that belong to the conveniency of the house, which would not have succeeded if they had been made entirely under ground, because the river is not far from it; but also that the order above might better enjoy the beautiful situation forwards.

Above the Doric portico rises an Ionic loggia, surmounted by mythological statues. Serving today as the civic art gallery, here you can enjoy daily (except on Sunday afternoons and Mondays) the Titians, Tintorettos and Tiepolos (not to mention works by Hans Memling and Anthony Van Dyck) that hang in the Palazzo Chiericati.

I relish the vaulted rooms of the building itself as much as these gorgeous paintings. 'All these vaults are adorned with most excellent compartments of stucco, by Messer BARTOLOMEO RIDOLFI, a *Veronese* sculptor; and paintings by Messer DOMENICO RIZZIO, and Messer BATTISTA VENETIANO, men singular in their profession,' wrote Palladio. Then, having praised others, Palladio described the rest of the interior, modestly contriving to praise his own ingenuity.

The hall is above in the middle of the front, and takes up the middle part of the loggia below. Its height is up to the roof; and because it projects forward a little, it has under the angles double columns. From one part to the other of this hall, there are two loggias, that is, on each side one; which have their soffits or ceilings adorned with very beautiful pictures, and afford a most agreeable sight.

The Teatro Olimpico must be one of the most unusual master-pieces in Italy. This was Palladio's last work, and although it was built within the short space of five years, he died before its completion by Scamozzi in 1584. The theatre is set in a garden, with statues of 1751 by G. Cassetti. Here, out of stucco and wood, the two architects created a remarkable three-dimensional stage, whose scenery, behind a Corinthian proscenium arch, re-creates in magical perspective a piazza and a classical street, with what appear to be five other streets running off to left and right. The main street is but twelve metres long, but brilliant tricks of perspective make it seem much longer.

The semicircular auditorium, under a 'sky' painted a hundred years ago, seats some 600 people, whose bodies absorb the echo from the stage. In truth, only those who sit at the centre of the semicircle appreciate the full beauty of the perspectives on the stage, though only those who walk to either end of the auditorium spot that there are not five, but seven, streets running off the main alleyway on the stage. Roman notables are here depicted, though forty of them represent the patrician members of the Nobilissima Accademia de' Signori Olimpici who paid for the building of this theatre. Francesco Maffei frescoed the theatre in 1635.

The first performance here in 1585 was of Sophocles' *Oedipus Rex*. From April to October the theatre is still the venue of plays, classical ballet and chamber music (but in winter the players and spectators would freeze to death, for to allow the place to be heated would risk burning down its fragile self).

Outside the theatre is a statue of the economist Fedele Lampertico, who lived from 1833 to 1906. This was a public-spirited man, as you will discover if you find time to follow the Corso Fogazzaro, which runs north-west from near the other end of Corso Andrea Palladio. This is another of those Vicenzan streets flanked by splendid palaces. The finest is no. 16, Palladio's Palazzo Valmarana, but the Bank of Italy deserves a mention and a pause, housed as it is in a baroque building of 1711 by F. Muttoni. It overlooks Piazza San Lorenzo, which is shaded by the church of the same name.

San Lorenzo is a brick, Gothic church, built for the Franciscans between 1280 and 1344. A Madonna and child, Saints Francis and Laurence, and busts of patriarchs, prophets and more saints enliven its portal, the work of Andriola de' Santi in 1344. The chubby fellow kneeling at the feet of the Madonna must, I guess, be the man who paid for it. The whole façade, with its blind arches, does not let down this superb marble portal. The cloister dates from the fifteenth century. Here you will discover a notice celebrating Fedele Lampertico's generosity in first buying, and then demolishing, a house that leaned against and obscured the view of this lovely basilica. Inside the church is a new monument, a bronze bust of St Maximilian Kolbe, a Polish Catholic priest who, as the bronze records, chose to die in a Nazi concentration camp in the place of a married man who, unlike Kolbe, had the responsibility of a wife and children.

A little range of volcanic mountains known as the Monti Bérici surrounds Vicenza. Clad with vegetation and vineyards, culminating in plateaux rather than summits, they shelter ancient farmhouses and villages. This is country for hiking and riding. Take the no. 8 bus, or drive south from the city by way of Porta Lupia, to find just outside Vicenza the Portici – which is a covered ascent of seventeen chapels and 150 arches flanking the Via X Giugno and designed by Muttoni in the second half of the eighteenth century – and also to visit the basilica of Monte Bérico. It stands on a spot where, twice in the plague years of 1426 to 1428, the Blessed Virgin Mary appeared to Vincenzo Pasini to assure him of her care for the city.

Today only its campanile dates from the original fifteenth-century building, a chapel which was replaced by Lorenzo da Bologna in 1476 with a building large enough to accommodate the increasing numbers of pilgrims. Lorenzo's sanctuary lasted scarcely a couple of centuries. The present baroque sanctuary, with its impressive dome, was rebuilt by Carlo Borella between 1688 and 1703, though the façade that Lorenzo da Bologna created now lines the south front.

Vicenza's finest sixteenth-century painter, Bartolomeo Montagna, contributed a moving *Pietà* to this sanctuary, but its greatest masterpiece is undoubtedly Veronese's 1572 'Supper of St Gregory the Great'. This is, however, scarcely the original painting. Troops of the Austrian Emperor Franz Josef slashed it to pieces in 1848, and the emperor paid for its restoration. Pilgrims do not, of course, come here primarily to see these works of art, but to venerate and plead before a 1444 statue of the Blessed Virgin.

The piazza offers a splendid panorama of the city of Vicenza and its hilly environs. Its name (Piazza della Vittoria) denotes its function as a First World War memorial. Below, some 500 metres away, stands Villa Valmarana dei Nani (the *nani* being the eighteen sculpted dwarfs that sit on its wall). You can visit this villa most afternoons from mid-March until mid-November. Antonio Muttoni's family began building it in 1669; his son Francesco finished it early in the next century.

Legend has it that the owner, whose daughter was born a dwarf, surrounded her with similar little people so that her infirmity would pass unnoticed. The villa's balustrade, monumental staircase, two-storeyed self and statue-topped portico are extremely beguiling; but its chief delights are the frescos by Giambattista Tiepolo and his son Giandomenico.

Just beyond the villa a path runs as far as another supreme

achievement of Palladio, the hilltop Villa Rotonda. From mid-March to mid-September you can visit the villa on Wednesday mornings, at other times exploring only the grounds and walking around the building. Villa Rotonda was begun in the mid-sixteenth century on behalf of Cardinal Almerico Capra and was finished by Scamozzi in 1606. It is perfectly symmetrical, a cube topped by a dome, with four classical porticoes, one located on each side, approached by magnificent staircases. In 1571 Rubini carved the statues above each pediment, while their reliefs are by Albanese.

Palladio well knew that he had created another masterpiece. 'Among the many honourable *Vicentine* gentlemen,' he wrote:

there is Monsignor PAOLO ALMERICO, an ecclesiastick, and who was referendary to two supreme Popes, PIO the fourth and fifth, and who for his merit, deserved to be made a *Roman* citizen with all his family. This gentleman after having travelled many years out of a desire of honour, all his relations being dead, came to his native country, and for his recreation retired to one of his country-houses upon a hill, less than a quarter of a mile distant from the city, where he had built according to the following invention: which I have not thought proper to place among the fabricks of villas, because of the proximity it has with the city, whence it may be said to be in the very city. The site is as pleasant and as delightful as can be found; because it is upon a small hill, of very easy access, and is watered on one side by the *Bacchiglione*, a navigable river; and on the other it is encompassed with most pleasing risings, which look like a very great theatre, and all are cultivated, and abound with most excellent fruits, and most exquisite vines: and therefore, as it enjoys from every part most beautiful views, some of which are limited, some more extended, and others that terminate with the horizon; there are loggias made in all the four fronts; under the floor of which, and of the hall, are the rooms for the conveniency and use of the family.

And Palladio continued:

The small rooms are divided off. Over the great rooms . . . there is a place to walk round the hall, fifteen foot and a half wide. In the extremity of the pedestals, that form a support to the stairs of the loggias, there are statues made by the hand of Messer LORENZO VICENTINO, a very excellent sculptor.

The northern environs of Vicenza are irresistible. Cittadella, twenty-two kilometres north-east of the city, is ringed with battle-mented walls, dating from the thirteenth and fourteenth centuries and encompassing thirty-two towers and four defensive gates. Formidable though they be, these walls are prettily patterned, with blind arches and white bands of Istrian stone. On Mondays the whole of this little circular city, with its regular criss-crossed streets, is packed with market stalls, some of them entirely devoted to selling shoes. The sixteenth-century Palazzo Pretorio is frescoed with Renaissance medallions and has a marble porch. The massive cathedral, rising in a wide piazza, has a Corinthian façade and inside is supported on Corinthian columns.

Look eastwards from here to a gateway, the Porta Bassanesi, whose tower has a fresco of the Carraresi escutcheon, which you will also see on a fortified gate at Castelfranco. Running in the other direction, the arcaded Via Garibaldi reaches a thirteenth-century tower, where steps rise to the thirteenth-century Porto Padova, a fortified double gateway with slits for the portcullis. Here, between the moat and the city wall, are a children's playground and Cittadella's public gardens.

Drive north from here to Bassano del Grappa, whose name derives renown both from the painter Jacopo da Ponte – otherwise known as Bassano, and born here in 1515 – and from the sweet aperitif Grappa. Bassano's 'Flight into Egypt' is, to my mind, the finest of his works in the Museo Civico, but here he has the misfortune to compete with paintings by Tiepolo and Longhi, as well as with sculptures by Canova. Bassano's love of the Venetian landscape appears in his brilliant painting of St Valentine baptizing St Lucy, whose silken robe glows luminously.

The first sight that impresses anyone entering Bassano del Grappa consists of the twin towers and octagonal cupola of the Tempio Ossario, a neat medieval pastiche that is a monument

59

to the dead of the Second World War. The street opposite this memorial leads to Piazza della Libertà, three sides of which are arcaded. In this piazza stand the column of St Bassano, erected in 1681, and a winged lion of 1518. The white façade of the church of San Giovanni Battista dates from its eighteenth-century renovation by Giorgio Miazzi, though the original building is fourteenth-century. Rising beyond the buildings of this piazza you can see the fourteenth-century Torre di Piazza. On the fifteenth-century Loggia del Commune, at the north-east corner of the piazza, is an astronomical clock made by G. da Molin in 1552, though its present mechanism was created in 1747.

To the east in Piazza Garibaldi is a dolphin fountain and the fourteenth-century church of San Francesco, its fanciful porch admitting you to a bare and dark interior. And from Piazza della Libertà, Via Giacomo Matteoti leads past the deconsecrated church of the Madonna (whose baroque façade is the work of B. Tabacco) to the twelfth-century Castello degli Ezzolini. On the way a plaque on the right of the street marks the birthplace of Giovanni Vaccari, dated MDCCCLXXI to MCMXIX.

The last time I was here, the thirteenth-century brick-built tower beside the *castello* supported vegetation, as did the brick campanile of the church of Santa Maria in Colle, which rises beyond it through an arch. A signpost now directs you downhill to Bassano del Grappa's chief curiosity, the Ponte degli Alpini. This thirteenth-century wooden bridge, covered and elegant, was restored by Palladio. The best view of the curious wooden stilts that support it is from the other side of the River Brenta, where you also discover the eighteenth-century Palazzo Sturm. Signs bring you back to the town centre by a different, picturesque route, which passes an eighteenth-century frescoed house and, in Piazzo Monte Vecchio, the fifteenth-century Monte di Pietà, whose façade has ancient coats of arms and is inscribed MONS PIETATIS.

Drive south-west to walled Maróstica, its arcaded houses set among cherry trees, chestnuts, olives and vines and guarded by two Scaliger castles and three fortified gates. Medieval walls climb from the lower town to the upper one. At one end of its main piazza stands the massive lower castle built by Cangrande, Lord of Verona, in 1311. Its courtyard is frescoed with star patterns and three saints: Antony Abbot, Christopher and a saint in a ship whom I take to be St Nicholas.

At the other end of the piazza is a modern building, though none the less decent, with a belfry and sundial. An old well and a column bearing a winged lion, dated MDLV (and placed here after Venice took control of Maróstica in 1504), adorn the square. But the oddity of this Piazza Castello is that it is paved like a chess board, for here on the first Sunday in September there takes place a chess match, in which men and women in fifteenth-century costume play the role of the pieces. The game dates from a contest between two suitors of Lionora, the daughter of Taddeo Parisio, lord of the *castello*, who forbade them to duel for her hand, instead making them contest her in a game of chess.

You climb through the olive groves to the upper castle by way of a couple of churches. The first, Sant'Antonio, was begun in the fourteenth century, has a medieval campanile and houses an altar painting by Bassano. Further on, at the foot of the Pausolino hill, the baroque church of the Carmine dates from 1694 to 1748.

This tour ends further south-west, at Thiene. An industrial town at the foot of the Asiago plateau and the start of the plain of Vicenza, Thiene is worth visiting for its seventeenth-century cathedral, with a coffered ceiling of 1769, its fifteenth-century Gothic brick church of the Natività, and, above all, for the Venetian Gothic Palazzo Thiene, otherwise known as the Castello da Porto Colleoni. Begun in 1476, the palace boasts mid-eighteenth-century stables by F. A. Muttoni, a Gothic chapel and mid-sixteenth-century frescos by Gian Battista Zelotti and Gianantonio Fasolo (it is open mid-March to mid-November on Sundays and holiday afternoons). The battlemented blocks at each end give a hint of past warfare, while the central block, rising from a portico with two graceful staircases, has delicate Venetian Gothic windows. While you are at Thiene, incidentally, do not miss Villa Beregan Cunico, built and stuccoed in the mid-seventeenth century, which can be visited in the mornings from Tuesday to Saturday if you phone in advance (0445-360923).

Intimations of past warfare remind one of a spiritual aim of these villas and their gardens, especially those designed by Palladio and his followers. Nature itself seemed to mirror the viciousness of previous years, when, instead of looking out of their windows on spacious vistas, people fearfully surrounded themselves with walls, inside which at dusk the farmers would lead their cattle, to shelter under formidable keeps.

Mindful of this, Renaissance landscape gardeners often set out to mimic the dangers from which they had so recently escaped. Sometimes they incorporated ruins in their gardens; at other times broken, leaning towers. Disjointed and sinister elements mingle with the Renaissance order that is seen as overcoming them. Nature is tamed, as had been the Dark Ages. Haphazard, unruly forests are cleared to become parks.

Palladio tamed nature more than any other architect. As you return to Vicenza, remember that his Villa Rotonda has no garden. On every side vineyards, woodlands and smooth fields rise right up to it. His ideal country home is surrounded by an immaculate, orderly, untangled landscape.

From Verona to Lake Garda

Apart from the Colosseum in Rome, the celebrated amphitheatre of Verona is the largest in Italy. Thirty-two metres high, 152 metres long and 128 metres wide, it was built in the first century AD to hold some 25,000 spectators. When you go in make sure to note which entrance you used. Especially out of the tourist season, I have sat on one of its pink and white stone seats (which were restored in the fifteenth century), brooding on its massive beauty, and then been unable to find my way out again. Walking perilously around the high perimeter of the arena, you spot that it was once even higher, for another huge section, three storeys tall and incorporating today eight great arches, rises from beyond the outer ring. (The rest collapsed in the earthquakes of 1117 and 1183.) As Goethe observed 200 years ago. 'The people of Verona deserve praise for preserving this monument. The pinkish marble of which it is built weathers badly, but as soon as the steps erode they repair them, so that nearly all of them seem brand-new.'

The greatest Venetan architects marvelled at this building. 'When the ancients had any very large fabrick to build, such as the *Arena* in *Verona*,' observed Palladio, 'to save time and

expence, they only wrought the imposts of the arches, the capitals
and cornices, leaving all the rest rustick, having regard only to the
beautiful form of the whole edifice.' Today, in the arena proper,
the great slabs of stone have been topped with brick, and parts
of the whole mended to provide for the modern open-air theatre,
which, since its inauguration in 1913, has been regarded (by the
citizens of Verona at any rate) as the most important opera theatre
in the world. The year 1913 was the centenary of the birth of
Verdi, and the first production in the Verona arena was fittingly
his *Aïda*.

This is also a spot from which to savour the environs of the
city. Joseph Addison, who visited Verona at the beginning of
the eighteenth century, exclaimed that 'The situation is the most
delightful I ever saw, it is so sweetly mixed with rising ground and
vallies, so elegantly planted with trees on which Bacchus seems
rising as it were in triumph every autumn, the vines reach from
tree to tree.' He added, 'Here of all places I have seen in Italy
would I fix a residence.'

The city predates its arena, which was built under the Emperor
Flavius in the first century AD. Verona's prehistoric importance
must have derived from the fact that the River Adige, which
makes beautiful loops through the city, could be forded, near
the present Ponte Pietra. Around this ford, which was important
for the amber and salt route from the Adriatic to Germany, the
Bronze Age tribes who lived here flourished. In the fourth century
BC their settlement was occupied by the Gallic Cenomani tribe
and became a colony of Rome in 49 BC, just after the death of
the greatest of Rome's lyric poets, Catullus, who had been born
here thirty-five years previously.

Just outside the city, in his drive to become the sole authority
in the Roman world, Constantine the Great defeated one of the
generals of his rival Maxentius in AD 312. The city embraced
Christianity when the Roman emperors decreed it one of the
religions of their realm, the citizens' faith deepened by the mis-
sionary work of St Zeno. Then, in the mid-fifth century, Verona

became the capital of the Ostrogothic kingdom, after Theodoric the Great defeated the barbarian leader Odoacer outside its walls. Theodoric built a fortress here beside the Adige, on the site today occupied by the Castel San Pietro.

The Lombards made Verona a dukedom. In 774 they were forced into submission by Pépin the Short, King of the Franks (and father of Charlemagne), who was crowned King of Italy in 781 and chose Verona as his Italian seat. Its mild climate attracted the eleventh-century theologian Berengar of Tours, whose attacks on the doctrine of transubstantiation led to his condemnation by Rome and his temporary excommunication.

Verona became part of the mark of Bavaria in the eleventh century, but soon achieved independence. As a free city, it espoused the Guelphs (the papal party) against the Ghibellines (the imperial party) and thus was a member of the alliance that defeated Barbarossa in 1164.

Less than a century later Verona was no longer free, dominated by Ezzolino of Romano (who managed to stop the feuds of great families by ruling as a tyrant from 1231 to 1259), and then by the della Scala family (the Scaligers), who ruled here from 1262 to 1387.

During the Scaliger hegemony, this family gained power over most of the Veneto, conquering Padua and threatening Treviso, as well as ruling considerable parts of Emilia and Tuscany. Its greatest scion, Cangrande I, gave refuge to Dante, who had been exiled from Florence in 1302 for his political activities. Dante obliquely thanked Cangrande with a fleeting reference in his *Paradiso:*

> *Ma tosta fia che Padova al palude*
> *cangerà l'acqua che Vicenza bagna,*
> *per esser al dover le genti crude.*

(The moment comes when, for their stubbornness,
 At Padua's marsh the water shall be changed
 That bathes Vicenza.)

– a reference to the defeat of Giacomo da Carrara by Cangrande outside Vicenza on 18 September 1314.

In 1386 Gian Galleazo Visconti supplanted the Scaligers as ruler of Verona. Next, the Viscontis were supplanted by the Carraresi family, and in 1405 the city fathers chose to submit to Venice. Apart from a few vicissitudes (in particular its occupation by the Emperor Maximilian I from 1509 to 1517), Verona remained under Venetian control until Napoleon destroyed the Venetian republic. In 1797, at Napoleon's behest, the treaty of Campio Formio ceded Verona to Austria.

In 1814, after a few years as a member of the kingdom of Italy, Verona was once again occupied by Austria, and remained Austrian until she finally joined the kingdom of Italy in 1866. And throughout these centuries the city nurtured great artists, above all Fra Giocondo, who introduced Renaissance art to Verona, and Paolo Caliari, who was born here in 1528 and took the name Veronese. Trained initially as a stone-cutter, Veronese conceived a passion for painting at the age of fourteen, as a pupil of Antonio Badile, whose daughter Elena he was soon to marry. And such was his talent that eventually Venice claimed him from his native city.

As we shall see, nearly every successive ruler and era has left its mark on the city. For a start, Piazza Brà, in which the arena stands, derives from the Austrian word *breit*, meaning 'wide'. Austria regarded Verona as an essential pillar of her defences, and between 1837 and 1842 Austrian military engineers built an impressive series of brick and tufa fortresses in the hills north of the city. They make a fascinating tour of ten kilometres or so, if you leave the city by car at Porta San Giorgio. The first fort you come across, Forte San Leonardo, was built in 1838 to shelter six guns and 180 soldiers. The next, Forte San Mattia, was built in the same year to accommodate eight guns and 368 troops. About 1,000 metres away stands Forte Sofia, which had fourteen guns and 174 men and is named after Sophie of Bavaria, the mother of the Austrian Emperor Franz Josef. In addition to these, Austrian engineers converted two existing Visconti fortresses for their own use, namely Castel San Pietro, which became a barracks in 1840, and Forte San Felice, which is a strengthened fourteenth-century castle, adding to these by fortifying the Venetian bastion known as the Rondella di Santa Toscana. Finally they built Forte Biondella, and the polygonal Batteria di Scarpa, which sheltered four guns and forty-two men.

To return to the Romans, the arena is but the greatest of their legacies to the city. A Veronese scholar named Scipione Maffei made a collection of Greek, Roman and medieval epigraphs which you can visit in the slightly pompous Maffeo museum in the Piazza Brà. Close by a little piazza is called the Mura di Galleno, because here stand Roman walls built by the emperor Gallienus in the mid-third century AD, while two fortified gateways, the dilapidated Porta Leona and the still-impressive Porta Borsari, both date from the time of Flavius. (The name of the second derives from the *bursarii*, the officers who collected the bishop's taxes.) The layout of the city still bases itself on the intersecting Roman streets, principally the *Cardus* (now Corso Sant'Anastasia and Corso Portoni Bosrari) and the *Decumanus* (now Via Leoni). And on the north-east side of the river, across a Roman bridge (the Ponte Pietra), stands a Roman theatre.

From the arena a pedestrianized narrow street runs north-east to join the lively Via Mazzini, filled with luxury shops and cafés. (Verona specializes in fashion and leather goods, particularly footwear.) Look out here for a notice that points towards the thirteenth-century Casa di Giuletta at no. 23 Via Capello. Verona is, of course, the city of Romeo and Juliet, and 'Capello' denotes Capulet, Juliet's family. Her (so-called) home has frescoed walls and splendid wooden ceilings, as well as a romantic balcony where, possibly, the ill-fated lovers had their most famous encounter. Juliet's tomb is said to be in a former Capuchin convent in Via del Pontiere outside the city walls, in whose Romanesque church of San Francesco al Corso the lovers are said to have married. In fact, all you are shown here (perhaps symbolic of the legend surrounding the whole tale) is an empty, red marble sarcophagus. Equally legendary (and delicious) are Verona's liqueur-filled chocolate *pasticcini* known as *baci di Giuletta*, or Juliet's kisses.

Returning to Via Mazzini, already you can see ahead the tallest tower in the city, the 84-metre-high Torre dei Lamberti with its two bells (the Rengo and the Marangona), which stands in the Piazza delle Erbe. This irregular piazza, which occupies the site of the ancient Roman forum, is an utterly delightful *mélange* of palaces and monuments. It opens up to reveal the striped, sandwich-cake design at the bottom of the Torre dei Lamberti, which was begun in 1172 and not finished until 1464, when the lantern was added. A lift takes you to the top. Here the daily fruit, vegetable and flower market sits, entirely at home, amid the old houses and towers of the square. Two hundred years ago Goethe noted that on market days the Veronese pile their stalls high with garlic, onions, vegetables and fruit, and then for the rest of the day shout, throw things, scuffle, laugh and sing. They still do.

The Piazza delle Erbe centres on a sixteenth-century marble pavilion with a fountain, under which the senators would once gather to issue decrees; on the Colonna del Mercato, which was set up in 1401; on a fountain created by Bonino da Campione in 1368 to carry a Roman statue (with a later head) known as Madonna Verona; and on the column of St Mark of 1523, on which a lion of St Mark has perched since 1888.

A bank now discreetly occupies the arcaded and crenellated Casa dei Mercanti of 1302, on which there is a Madonna sculpted by Girolamo Campagna in 1595. Its simple, round arches exude contentment. Beyond the column of St Mark, statues prance on the baroque Palazzo Maffei, which was built in 1668 and rubs shoulders with the Gardello tower of 1370. On the other side of the piazza 400-year-old frescos decorate houses built between the fourteenth and sixteenth centuries and enlivened with curving wrought-iron balconies. On the same side the Arco della Costa, an arch dating from 1470, joins the massive Palazzo del Commune (originally built in 1193, but rebuilt in the last century) with the Domus Nova of 1659.

Through the Arco della Costa (so named from the whale's rib hanging from it) and a second Renaissance arch you reach the magnificent Piazza dei Signori, with its 1865 monument to a pensive Dante who, as we have seen, took refuge in Verona from his enemies in the early fourteenth century (and helped to inspire the Scaligers' dream of restoring the empire). Here the south-west façade of the Domus Nova is far finer than the façades we have already seen, and beyond it lies a Renaissance well. The arch beside it has a 1756 statue of the Veronese dramatist Scipione Maffei, who lived from 1675 to 1755. A field marshal as well as a playwright, his most successful work was the tragedy *Merope*, written in 1713.

Back in the piazza, over an archway is the statue of the Scaligers' doctor, Aventino Frascatoro, set here in 1559. His arch is linked to the extremely graceful Venetian Renaissance Loggio del Consiglio, built (probably by Fra Giocondo da Verona) between 1476 and 1493. Twin windows, stucco-work, polychrome decoration and, above all, statues add to the grace of this building – the statues created by Alberto da Milano in 1483 and representing Catullus, Pliny, Macrinus, Vitruvius and Cornelius Nepos. Every detail of this building is delicate, especially the decoration of its pilasters.

On the opposite side of the square, the courtyard of the Palazzo del Commune, with its row of triple-lighted mullioned windows, is finely decorated with Romanesque bands of brick and stone. A spacious and extremely fine fifteenth-century staircase climbs two sides of the courtyard. This palace is linked by an arch to the Palazzo del Capitano, with its crenellated fourteenth-century tower, its sixteenth-century façade, a porch of 1530 by Michele Sanmicheli and, in the courtyard, the ostentatiously baroque Porta Bobardiera, created by Miglioranzi in 1687.

The Scaliger family lived in the thirteenth-century Palazzo del Governo at the far end of the piazza. Its doorway was added by Sanmicheli in 1532, an elaborate Doric affair, with sculpted ladies, wreaths and laurels. The lion of St Mark stands proudly above this doorway, and rightly so, for Sanmicheli was Venice's favoured architect in transforming Verona into a fortified city, when she became the vassal of La Serenissima. In the palazzo's courtyard is a Renaissance well and a sixteenth-century loggia frescoed by Altichiero. Both Giotto and Dante found shelter in this palace.

The Scaliger family worshipped in the twelfth-century Romanesque church of Santa Maria Antica, which rises across the street from their palace. Inside and out this is a delightful little rustic church, whose tower has a pointed cap. In its tiny square stands the Scaligers' mausoleum, the Arche Scaligere. Bonino da Campione was responsible for the tomb of Cangrande I, who died in 1329, and here too stands a copy of the remarkable equestrian statue of an enigmatically smiling Cangrande himself, whose sculptor remains anonymous. (The fourteenth-century original is in the art museum.) The Scaliger rebus (a staircase or *scala*) repeats itself in the fourteenth-century forged-iron railing around their other tombs, which include the sarcophagus of Mastino I, founder of the dynasty (who was assassinated in the Piazza dei Signori in 1277); two other tombs (that of Mastino II, who died in 1351, and of Cansignorio, who died in 1375) by Bonino da Campione; and two more (of Alberto I, who died in 1301, and Giovanni della Scala, who died in 1359) by Andreolo de' Santi.

Here Romeo and Juliet put in a second appearance, for in Via delle Arche Scaligere to the right a Gothic house with a brick façade once belonged to the Montecchi family and is now called the Casa di Romeo. It is inscribed with the Bard's own words: 'O where is Romeo . . . I have lost myself, I am not here. This is not Romeo, he's some other where.'

From the corner of this street, take Via Santa Maria in Chiavica and turn left along Via San Pietro Martire to find the huge, red brick Gothic church of Santa Anastasia, which the Dominicans built between 1290 and 1323 and again between 1423 and 1481, when they finished the slender, terracotta-decorated campanile.

The sculpted twin portal dates from the fourteenth century. On its right pillar two terracotta tablets depict the life of St Peter Martyr. Dark, high, impressive and frescoed by Pisanello, the interior of Santa Anastasia (its plan a Latin cross) is far from displaying Dominican simplicity. Two giants groan under its fonts. Pisanello's 'St George rescuing the princess of Trebizond from the dragon', painted in 1436, is the undoubted masterpiece in this church; but do not neglect, for example, the work of Giotto's follower Altichiero ('The Cavalli family, presented to the Blessed Virgin Mary by three saints', painted in 1395) or Liberale da Verona's fifteenth-century 'Deposition'.

The church of San Pietro Martire next to Santa Anastasia is now an art gallery. It was built by Giovanni Falconetto and consecrated in 1354. Peter Martyr was a Veronese Dominican who pursued the cause of the inquisition with such ferocity that the people of Como killed him in 1251. The church was formerly dedicated to St George, until the Dominicans assigned it to their own saint and martyr, but St George himself appears over the lunette in a fresco by Jacopo Ligozzi (1547–1626). The church also boasts frescos that depict the blessed Virgin Mary in a walled garden, taming a unicorn (a symbol of wildness brought to heel by purity). One of the other garden residents seems to me to be a dodo. Outside the church, in a tomb on an arch, sleeps Bavarino Crescenzi, another physician to the Scaligers, who died in 1346.

Walk around the polygonal apse of Santa Anastasia, which overlooks the River Adige. A plaque on a wall reveals the alarming level of flooding on 12 September 1872, and further upstream you can see the medieval gateway and the stone and brick arches of the Ponte Pietra, part Roman, part medieval and scrupulously rebuilt from the original materials after being mined in 1945.

Go back down Via Ponte Pietra and turn right along Via Duomo towards the cathedral. On the left stands Palazzo Forte, which Ignazio Pellegrini built at the end of the eighteenth century on the site of a twelfth-century palace (part of which has been excavated). Today the palace is the museum of modern art and of the Risorgimento.

Beside the cathedral stands the episcopal palace of 1502. This Vescovado has a Venetian Renaissance façade and statues (some of them perhaps by the Olivetan monk Fra Giocondo da Verona) of the Madonna and Saints Peter, Paul and Michael. The bishops clearly felt the need at times for self-protection and preserved the battlemented Romanesque keep, built by Bishop Ognibene in 1172, which dominates their palace. The portico is also Romanesque.

The bishops would leave their palace to relish the superb twelfth-century Romanesque apse of their cathedral, in striped brick and marble. On the right rises the Renaissance campanile, built by Sanmicheli on a Romanesque base (apart from the bell-chamber, which was added in the 1920s). The cathedral's west façade is terrific. Santa Maria Matricolare replaced a temple of Minerva here in 1187 and cannibalized some of its stones. In the twelfth century a certain Master Niccolò sculpted the reliefs of its portal. Twisted columns rise from Romanesque griffins. Figures huddle in the pilasters of the doorway. Two knights guard the entrance, while above the door sits a sculpted Romanesque Virgin Mary, attended by shepherds and the Magi.

In the fifteenth century much of the building was Gothicized. The organ case is a gilded baroque treat. In 1534 Sanmicheli built the marble balustrade which surrounds the choir. Even greater artists added their gifts to Verona's cathedral: in 1527 Jacopo Sansovino created the Nicholesa tomb in the first chapel of the north aisle; and for this chapel Titian painted a superb 'Assumption'. Newly cleaned when last I knelt before it, the painting glows with four different reds. Some of the onlookers are peering into the tomb, seeking the body of the vanished Virgin. Others have spotted that she is now in heaven. And the Virgin herself, in a deep ultramarine robe, looks compassionately down.

The cathedral cloister remains Romanesque, its twin columns

built in the mid-twelfth century, its pavement of mosaic (some of it, uncovered by archaeologists, dating from the sixth century AD). Two adjacent neighbouring churches date from the same era as the cloisters: Santa Elena, which stands on the site of the city's eighth-century cathedral, and San Giovanni in Fonte, which has preserved eleventh-century capitals and a late eleventh-century font with eight delicate bas-reliefs. This is the cathedral's baptistry, and eighth-century columns and capitals, survivors from the earlier cathedral, support the atrium that leads to it.

This part of Verona is entrancingly sprinkled with Gothic and Renaissance palaces, and you wind through them to reach the frescoed church of Santa Eufemia, which was built for the Augustinians in 1262, altered in 1375 and has a porch of 1486. Walk on along Via Emilei, turn left down Via Diaz when you reach the river again, and you arrive at Corso Cavour, with its Gothic, Renaissance and baroque palaces. It also contains the Romanesque apse, tower and cloister of the church of Santi Apostoli, built in 1194 over the subterranean church of Santi Tosca e Teuteria, which dates from 751. You reach this second venerable building, which now serves as a burial chapel, by steps from the sacristy.

Beyond it lies Sanmicheli's finest work in Verona, the Palazzo Bevilacqua, which he built in 1530. Opposite, through an archway with a statue of St Laurence, is a humbler house of God, but one still able to match Sanmicheli's in grace. The church of San Lorenzo is an early twelfth-century Romanesque building with cylindrical towers and a three-naved interior, decorated with alternating bands of tufa and brick.

The first-century AD Arco dei Gavi, a Roman archway designed by Verona's son Vitruvius Cedone (pulled down in 1805 and brilliantly reconstructed in 1932), heralds two fine monuments bequeathed to Verona by Cangrande II. The first is the 120-metre-long bridge, which here spans the Adige. The second is the towered, castellated and moated Castelvecchio, which was begun in 1354 and many times restored and enlarged. Both fortress and bridge were built for the Scaligers at a moment when their power was under threat.

Strategically, the bridge was designed to facilitate the route to Germany, for in the struggle between Guelph and Ghibelline, the Scaligers were Ghibellines, supporters of the Holy Roman Emperor. Today their fortress houses the civic museum, with paintings by such masters as Tintoretto, Veronese, Bellini, Verona's native painter Liberale, and Rubens. Veronese's 'Deposition', which came from the Verona church of St Fermo, is probably his earliest-known work; and here you can see the equestrian statue of Cangrande I that once topped his tomb.

The Adige swings northwards here. You have the choice of following it along the quayside, passing the little thirteenth-century church of San Zeno in Orotorio, to reach the magnificent church of San Zeno Maggiore, or else continuing due west to find the entrancing church of San Bernardino, built in the mid-fifteenth century and half-Gothic, half-Renaissance in style. Inside this building, the *cappella pellegrini* of 1557 is by Sanmicheli, the organ dates from 1481, and charming frescos by Niccolò Giolfino show views of Verona as it was when he painted them in 1522.

St Zeno, who died around 380, well deserves two churches in Verona. For one thing, he championed the unfashionable virtue of patience, describing it as 'the support of virginity, the secure harbour of widowhood, the guide and directress of the married state, the unanimity of friendship, and the comfort and joy of slavery'. Second, some two centuries after his death he performed a remarkable miracle. In 589 the Adige overflowed, threatening to drown most of Verona. As the eighteenth-century hagiographer Alban Butler put it:

The people flocked in crowds to the church of their holy patron, Zeno: the waters seemed to respect its doors, they gradually swelled as high as the windows, yet the flood never broke into the church, but stood like a firm wall, as when the Israelites passed the Jordan; and the people remained there twenty-four hours in prayer, till the waters subsided within the banks of the channel.

Built for the Benedictines, San Zeno Maggiore, one of Italy's finest Romanesque churches, dates back to the eighth century. Apart from its campanile, which was built between 1045 and 1149, the present building was begun in the first half of the twelfth century and was finished by 1225. A new apse was built in the late fourteenth century. One measure of its importance in the Middle Ages is that Alberto of Verona made his illegitimate son abbot of the monastery of San Zeno, for which Dante (who described the abbot as 'born in sin, ill-made in body and worse in mind') consigned Alberto to Purgatory.

Its west façade, which overlooks a piazza with the campanile and the Torre del Re Pipino of around 1300, is even finer than that of the cathedral. In the tympanum St Zeno conquers Satan. The porch, sculpted by a master named Niccolò in 1138, rises from a couple of lions and is embellished by scenes from scripture and allegory, as well as by the celebrated carving of the Emperor Theodoric hunting a stag. Superb bronze reliefs of biblical scenes adorn the eleventh-century bronze doors, the left panels depicting the Old Testament, the right the New. And above is a rose window depicting the wheel of fortune.

Inside, alternating piers and columns (some with Roman capitals) support a complex, wooden barrel vault carved in 1386. Another Roman borrowing is a porpyhry font. Fifteenth-century stalls, frescos and a twelfth-century font carved from pink marble add to one's pleasure, while in no way interfering with the superb spaciousness of the interior. In 1459 Mantegna painted a triptych for this church, depicting the Virgin Mary and eight saints; but its wings have been stolen and now hang in the museum of Tours and the Louvre. St Zeno's statue dates from the thirteenth century. The crypt, where his body lies in a nineteenth-century tomb, is borne by forty-nine Romanesque columns. And on the north side of the great church is a cloister begun in 1123 and finished in the fourteenth century.

The stern calm of San Zeno Maggiore is annually disturbed during the February carnival at Verona. On the Friday of the festival, allegorical floats, characters wearing traditional ancient masks (the god Bacchus, the god of gold, Papà del Gnocco) and others in more modern, fanciful outfits parade through the streets. The procession ends in the piazza of San Zeno, where everyone eats *gnocchi* made from potatoes, flour and water and covered with melted butter and parmesan cheese.

Nearby this church, as part of the fortifications that Sanmicheli planned for Verona in 1541, stands the Porta San Zeno. Further south is another of his fortified gateways, the finest of four that survive, the Porta Palio. Giorgio Vasari declared it the most beautiful in Italy. And if you continue along Circonvalazzione from the Porta Palio you will reach the third of his splendid gates, the Porta Nuova. From here walk north back to the arena. Just before it you come upon two battlemented arches, which remain from the Visconti fortifications of 1389, as well as the Gran Guardia, an imposing palace built by Sanmicheli's pupil D. Curtoni in 1610. Today the Visconti arches have been humanized with a clock, and beside them rises a pentagonal tower built by the tyrant Ezzolino.

Sanmicheli's fourth Verona gateway, the Porta San Giorgio of 1525 (which some in fact ascribe to Falconetto), is situated on the other side of the river, beyond the cathedral and near the impressive church of San Giorgio in Braida, for which he designed the dome and campanile (though he never finished the second, and no one else has thought to do so). The other glory of the church is its paintings: works by Jacopo and Domenico Tintoretto and, above all, Veronese's 'Martyrdom of St George' on Sanmicheli's high altar. As Goethe opined, 'San Giorgio is an art gallery'.

Walk east along Largo San Giorgio to find Castel San Pietro, part of the Visconti fortifications of the city (though its present form dates mostly from the nineteenth century, when it served as the Austrian barracks). The castle and the quiet Romanesque church of Santi Siro e Libera overlook the Roman theatre, which dates from the time of Augustus Caesar and abuts on to a convent, which today serves as Verona's archaeological museum. Since

1948 the Roman theatre has been the venue of Verona's annual Shakespeare festival.

Not far away stands the twelfth-century church of Santo Stefano. From here there is a delicious view across the river to the cathedral and the episcopal palace. A succession of treats – the wooded, terraced Giusti gardens, which were laid out in the sixteenth century around the Palazzo Giusti; Santa Maria in Organo, a church founded in the seventh century, though rebuilt in the late fifteenth (with a campanile built by the monk Fra Giocondo da Verona in the 1520s, and inside his superb marquetry stalls, lectern and candelabrum); the church of Santi Nazaro e Celso, built between 1463 and 1484; and Sanmicheli's Palazzo Pompei (now the city's natural science museum) – takes you south to the Ponte Navi, so called because it was once a bridge made of boats. Before crossing it, spare a glance at the sixteenth-century Porta Vescovi, a little way east, so named because the bishops charged a toll for passing through it. Sanmicheli's pupils designed the original Porta Vescovi, but the present one was fortified by the Austrians.

Then cross the bridge for one last Veronese church, San Fermo Maggiore, built for a Franciscan convent from the eleventh to the fourteenth centuries. This is a quaint building, in two distinct halves. Because it took so long to construct, the lower part of the church is Romanesque, the upper Gothic. The Scaliger physician Aventino Frascatoro, who died in 1368, lies entombed beside the entrance. Why did these distinguished men prefer to be buried outside rather than inside churches? The ceiling of this church, like the upturned keel of a ship, dates from the thirteenth and fourteenth centuries. Antonio da Mestre designed the marble pulpit in 1396. Pisanello painted an 'Annunciation' for the church (over the funeral monument, which the Florentine Nanni di Bartolo designed for Niccolò Brenzoni in 1439), and the choir screen dates from 1573. This complex building has a double cloister with seventeenth-century frescos. And from it Via Leoncino leads back to Piazza Brà.

*

Verona is shaded to the north by the high plain of the Lessini mountains, which are celebrated by speleologists for the subterranean cavity known as the Spluga della Preta: by palaeontologists for the vast number of fossils discovered here (many of them now in the museum at Bolca, from which you can walk to visit the caves in which some were found); and by naturalists for its flora and fauna. Here is the Ponte di Vejam, the largest natural bridge in Europe. And Lessinia boasts fifty kilometres of downhill slopes, served by two chair-lifts and seventeen ski-lifts. Here too are some forty kilometres of cross-country runs, and the region is favoured by horseback riders. Camp sites and hotels, as well as holiday flats and *pensiones*, accommodate the energetic.

High pastures, hills strewn with cherry and chestnut trees, and vast forests cover this peaceful region, which is dotted by stone farms, villages and patrician houses, and dissected by five valleys: Valpantena, Val di Squaranto, Val d'Illasi, Val d'Alpone and the celebrated vine-clad slopes of Valpolicella.

The extent of these vineyards never fails to surprise, and the nose of their wine always adds an especial delight to a tour of the towns and villages of this region. Valpolicella seems to me perfect for washing down the garlic-pricked pork that is a speciality of the region. But these places have other charms too. Arbizzano, for instance, eight kilometres north-west of Verona, has a thirteenth-century church, inside which is a fourteenth-century triptych and a fifteenth-century octagonal font. This is villa country too, scattered with the splendid residences of Verona's nobility, who derived their wealth from their huge estates outside the city.

At Pedemonte, three kilometres away from Arbizzano, Palladio designed the Villa Boccoli-Serego in 1566 (though others added their less skilled hands to its building). At San Ambrogio di Valpolicella near Gargagnano you can visit (on Tuesday and Thursday afternoons in summer and Thursday mornings in winter) the fourteenth-century house now known as Villa Serego Alighieri, which was the home of Dante's son Pietro Alighieri. Also at San Ambrogio di Valpolicella is mined the red marble that enhances so many fine homes in Verona. Eight kilometres north from here is San Giorgio, whose Romanesque church – though restored in the thirteenth century – is venerable enough to house an eighth-century ciborium, some fragmentary frescos and an octagonal baptistry.

Nearby at Fumane, if you telephone in advance, you can see Villa dell Torre Cazzola, a mid-sixteenth-century villa, perhaps by Sanmicheli, perhaps by Giulio Romano, with an ingeniously watered garden. And further west at Volargne, which gives you entry to the narrow Rivoli gorge of the River Adige, is the fifteenth- and sixteenth-century Villa del Bene, with eighteenth-century frescos by G. Caroto and D. Brusasorci and a portal by Sanmicheli (open daily except on Mondays).

To return slightly east, to the heart of the wine country, San Floriano boasts a twelfth-century Romanesque church, while near the wine centre of San Pietro in Cariano is Villa della Torre, which was probably designed by Sanmicheli. As for the cluster of villas near Negrar, a mere seven kilometres north-west of Verona, one of these has its place in this book in the chapter devoted to Venetan villas in general (see p.39).

Roveré Veronese, 843 metres above sea-level, is the principal summer and winter sports centre of the Val di Squaranto. In the Valpantena the local capital, 1,106-metre-high Bosco Chiesanuova, co-ordinates the activities of tourists, hikers and those who relish winter sports. From Bosco Chiesanuova a chair-lift rises to the 1,494-metre-high Malga San Girgio.

South-east of here at Illasi, in the Val d'Illasi, stand two magnificent early eighteenth-century villas: Villa Carlotti of 1735 (which you can see only from the outside) and Villa Perez Pompei Sagramoso of 1737, both of them richly decorated and furnished, the second particularly grand. The great central building and the two wings of Villa Perez Pompei Sagramoso were designed by G. B. Pozzo and, in the 1740s, by A. Mela and G. B. Cignaroli, before Andrea Porta crowned their work in the 1780s with some splendid mythological scenes. (For a visit you must telephone in advance:

045-7834062.) In this valley too is Giazza, with its ethnographic museum. And at Tregano, six kilometres north of Illasi, you can visit (telephone 045-7808127) the eighteenth-century Villa Pellegrini, with its rococo stucco and frescos by Porta.

The medieval town of Soave has a name redolent of wine. It lies east of Verona in the Val d'Alpone, by way of Caldiero, a spa of hot sulphurous waters. The Scaliger family built the crenellated walls of Soave in the fourteenth-century, reinforcing them with twenty-four towers, which climb up to the fortress that overlooked the spot even before the time of the Scaligers. The Venetians also added to the fortifications in 1413, and built Soave's Gothic Palazzo Cavalli in 1411, while Soave's medieval town hall dates from 1375 and its parish church has a 1529 painting of the Madonna by Fra Morone.

Wine then is not the only attraction of this part of the province. South-east of Soave lies the industrial town of San Bonifácio, which boasts the Romanesque church of San Abbonidio, which was frescoed in the fifteenth century. The suburb of Villanova di San Bonifácio has an even finer church. Here stands the twelfth-century abbey-church of San Pietro Apóstolo, built over an earlier crypt with pretty capitals. It once served a Benedictine monastery. The belfry of its campanile was added in the very late fourteenth century, when the monks also sculpted the frieze on the north side. In the eighteenth century they transformed the interior in the baroque fashion, without destroying the late fourteenth-century frescos depicting the life of St Benedict in the south aisle. A fifteenth-century sandstone altar is decorated with saints, while the high altar has an eighth-century relief.

Further east is Lonigo, where a miracle-working image of the Blessed Virgin Mary prompted the citizens to employ Lorenzo da Bologna to enlarge their monastery church in the 1480s. In consequence you can now enjoy its impressively rich façade, before visiting Lonigo's *rocca*, which is really a villa (and is sometimes called Villa Pisani), built by Scamozzi in the late 1570s and modelled on Palladio's Villa Rotonda. Lonigo's Palazzo

Communale was built by Sanmicheli in 1557. And a couple of kilometres north-east from here, at Sarego, stands the Villa da Posto, known as 'La Favorita', built by F. A. Muttoni in 1715 and frescoed by J. Guarana.

South-west of Verona the province is also well worth exploring. Washed by the River Tione, Villafranca di Verona is guarded by a castle built for the Scaligers in the thirteenth and fourteenth centuries, and whose keep and chapel are still intact. Here, on 10 November 1859, the Emperors Franz-Josef and Napoleon III signed the treaty that ended the costly Italian campaign which had set Austria and France at odds.

South-east at Grezzano is the splendid baroque Villa Allegri Arvedi, built in 1656 by G. C. Bianchi, decorated with Doric and Attic half-columns and topped with statues. The interior, which has a small chapel, contains frescoes of 1717 to 1720 depicting mythical personages and beasts by L. Dorigny. The garden is as magnificent as the house, its fountain another ingenious device to water the rest. (To visit the villa, telephone 045-907145.) Another Scaliger castle, this one in ruins, rises to the north-west at Valéggio sul Mincio, whose medieval bridge, built in 1393 to cross the Mincio, is also in ruins. Nearby is the early eighteenth-century Villa Maffei Della Quercia Sigurtà, with its spacious, exquisite gardens and 50-hectare park (which alone you can visit). Between the two towns is Custoza, whose wines should by no means be neglected.

Lake Garda constitutes the western boundary of the Veneto. Its northernmost town, Torbole, lies in the province of Trento; but everyone who wishes to explore the eastern side of this lake, which is dubbed the *olive riviera*, should start at Torbole, if only because on 12 September 1786, while in Italy editing his *Iphigenie*, Goethe arrived here and was entranced. In those days Torbole was not even the fishing village that it has but recently outgrown. In Goethe's words, it was merely a landing harbour. His lodging lacked what he called 'an extremely necessary convenience'. 'Qui abasso può servirsi! Dove?' he asked the servant. 'Da per tutto, dove vuol!' came the friendly reply. After this Goethe tucked into the salmon-like trout of the lake and finished his meal with delicious figs and pears. He looked out of his inn and saw both shores of the lake, bordered by hills and mountains that glimmered with the lights from countless small villages.

Two days later, and sixteen kilometres further south, Goethe was almost arrested at Malcesine. Today you reach Malcesine by means of a road that occasionally tunnels through the foothills of Monte Altissimo di Nago, at 2,078 metres one of the highest peaks of the Baldo massif. A cable-car takes sportsmen and -women to Tratto Spino (1,780 metres above sea-level). Boats ply the lake, which here washes the isles of Sogno, Olivo and Trimelone.

Malcesine is guarded by a Scaliger fortress, built in the thirteenth and fourteenth centuries. Today the keep serves as a little museum of the lake region. Malcesine's Renaissance town hall once served the captains of the lake, who controlled the traffic on behalf of Verona. Olives grow on the slopes of Monte Baldo behind the town. And here, as a plaque recalls, Goethe, sketching the fortress, was taken for an Austrian spy. An unprepossessing official approached him, asked what he was doing and peremptorily tore up the page of his drawing sheet. A crowd had gathered by now, and many seemed displeased at this high-handed behaviour, especially one old woman, who told Goethe to call the *Podestà*. This worthy turned out to be almost as dull-witted as the first official. The fortress, he insisted, stood on the frontier between Austria and the Veneto, and thus no one should spy on it. His aide observed that the Austrian emperor had evil designs on the republic of Venice. Finally Goethe revealed that he was a citizen of Frankfurt-am-Main, at which his allies in the crowd called up a 50-year-old man who had once served in that city. He speedily persuaded the authorities that Goethe was innocent and, what is more, that evening he invited the sage to his vineyard, where they sampled the finest grapes.

At Brenzone, further south, is a twelfth-century Romanesque church dedicated to St Zeno, while its sister village Assenza has a fourteenth-century church (in which are contemporary frescos) dedicated to St Nicholas of Bari. Torri del Benaco, another fishing village turned tourist resort, is the next stop on this shore of Lake Garda. Once again the Scaligers defended it with a fortress, this one built in 1388, but dominating the whole is the massive mountain. Torri del Benaco, with its castle and its harbour in which yachts nestle, guards the approach to the promontory of San Vigilio. Sports fanatics take off from here to San Zeno di Montagna. The picturesque promontory is rendered even more charming by its ancient cypresses and its sixteenth-century Villa Guarienti Brenzone, built by Sanmicheli. Just around the promontory lies Garda itself, its medieval *rocca* in ruins, its narrow streets typical of these lakeside towns. Here is an eighteenth-century church with a fifteenth-century campanile and a fifteenth-century cloister. The *rocca* is old enough to have served as a prison for Queen Adelaide, incarcerated here by Berengar II after the death of her husband Lothair of Italy in 950. (Happily, she escaped.)

As one travels south, the mountains of the hinterland begin to give way to gentler hills. Bardolino is as famous as Valpolicella for its wines, but the Venetans also cherish its olives and fruit. The spot is ancient, witness its ninth-century Carolingian church of St Zeno, its medieval houses and the twelfth-century Romanesque church of San Severo, with a fine campanile and an apse frescoed in the thirteenth century.

Beyond Bardolino, Lazise is still surrounded by medieval walls, some of its walks shaded by palm trees, its temporal peace symbolically guaranteed by the Scaliger fortress, its spiritual peace cared for by a thirteenth-century, frescoed church dedicated to St Nicholas, patron saint of sailors. Here too is a sixteenth-century Venetian customs house.

The eastern side of Lake Garda ends at Peschiera, where the waters of the lake run out into the River Mincio. Peschiera was part of the Austrian 'Quadrilateral', that series of fortifications which included the fortresses we have explored at Verona. In consequence, here the Austrians pulled down Peschiera's medieval castle and built a new fortress. The Scaligers seem to have been particularly anxious to protect their territory in this region. Secure in the north, because of their alliance with the German emperors, they guarded the southern Veronese plains with the fortresses of Salizzole, Sanguinetto and Isola Della Scala (of which only the tower remains). And around the River Mincio in the mid-fourteenth century they devised an even more powerful defensive system. A 16-kilometre-long series of walls and towers known as *Il Serraglio* – now almost entirely disappeared but beginning with the mighty ruins of the Ponte Visconteo at Borghetto sul Mincio, a bridge built across the river in 1393 – linked the fortresses of Valéggio sul Mincio, Villafranca and Nogarole Rocca.

Lake Garda is noted for its mild climate, which encourages palm trees, cypresses, olives, lemons and cedars to flourish on its shores. It can also be fickle. In 1709 the lake froze completely. Virgil's *Georgics* (which call the lake Benacus) note that the waters become stormy in winter:

> Here vex'd by winter storms Benacus raves,
> Confus'd with working sands and rolling waves;
> Rough and tumultuous like a sea it lies,
> Loud the tempest roars, so high the billows rise.

(The translation is Dryden's.)

But today the chief danger around the eastern shore of Lake Garda seems to me to derive from inexperienced hang-gliders. Altogether the lake exults in fifty kilometres of clean beaches, nearly all of them sheltered by the surrounding hills and mountains. The lake is also a haven for windsurfers, water-skiers and fishermen. Steamboats ply the lake; fishing boats and pleasure craft tie up peacefully in its harbours.

I first stayed on the shores of Lake Garda at the age of seventeen, when hang-gliding and windsurfing were non-existent. Even then I was romantic enough to learn by heart one of Tennyson's poems as I sat in a rowing boat by the beach. In it Tennyson paid tribute to Catullus, whose villa was at Sirmione on Lake Garda and whose unrequited love inspired some passionate poetry. As Tennyson wrote:

Row us out from Desenzano, to your Sirmione row!
So they row'd, and there we landed – 'O venusta Sirmio!'
There to me thro' all the groves of olive in the summer glow,
There beneath the Roman ruin where the purple flowers grow,
Came that 'Ave atque Vale' of the Poet's hopeless woe,
Tenderest of Roman poets nineteen-hundred years ago,
'Frater Ave atque Vale' – as we wander'd to and fro
Gazing at the Lydian laughter of the Garda Lake below
Sweet Catullus's all-but-island, olive-silvery Sirmio!

Rovigo and the Po valley

The column bearing the lion of St Mark in Piazza Vittorio Emanuele II at Rovigo is older than the sculpted beast itself, dating from 1519, whereas the lion that tops it was set here only in 1881; yet it fittingly symbolizes the history of this city, for in 1482 Niccolò III, Lord of Este, sold Rovigo to Venice for 50,000 ducats.

Four centuries previously the city was already a flourishing centre of trade. The inhabitants protected their homes by encircling their pentagonal city with walls in the twelfth century. The first persons to lord it over their fellow-citizens in the Middle Ages were the bishops of Rovigo, but soon their rule was replaced by that of the Estensi family of Ferrara. Today one can still trace the medieval pattern of Rovigo that they dominated, in the arcaded streets which lead from Piazza Vittorio Emanuele to the city gates, though it is as well to do so on foot, for although Rovigo has all the bustle of a modern Italian city, there are quiet places where the car cannot venture.

The oldest parts of Rovigo, the towered walls and the ruins of the tenth- to twelfth-century castle, which was founded by Bishop

Paolo Cataneo of Adria in 920, are an evocative reminder of the stern face of the Middle Ages. The Torre Municipale survives from the defences of 1138 and, of the two surviving city gates, the finest, the twelfth-century Porta San Bartolomeo, recalls the Venetian triumph over Rovigo, for it was strengthened by the new masters of the city in the 1480s. (The Donà delle Rose family added its coat of arms to the gateway in the sixteenth century.) The second gate, the Porta di Sant'Agostino, was rebuilt in 1713. Of the surviving castle towers (both of them leaning), the Torre Mozza and the Torre Donà (named after the eighteenth-century owners of the fortress), the second is the tallest and the oldest, dating back to the time when Rovigo was continually assaulted by the Hungarians. (The bronze statue in front of them is to the anti-Fascist martyr Giacomo Matteotti, who was murdered on 10 June 1924.) And in the public gardens there still rise a couple of once-fearsome tenth-century towers.

Lovely buildings surround Piazza Vittorio Emanuele II (which centres on a marble monument to that monarch, bemedalled and wearing baggy trousers, sculpted in 1881 by Giulio Monteverdi). They include the sixteenth-century Palazzo del Municipio, over whose triple portico is a loggia carrying a 1690 statue of the Madonna and child by Giuliano Mauro (while, inside, its treasures include a sixteenth-century 'Ecce Homo' by Antonio Aleotti and a seventeenth-century *Pietà* by Francesco Maffei); the Palazzo Roverella, with its columns and gentle Gothic courtyard, designed by the Ferraran architect Biagio Rossetti in 1472; the Palazzo Roncale (to the left of the Palazzo del Municipio in Via Laurenti), built by Sanmicheli in 1555; and the mid-eighteenth-century Torre dell'Orologio, an unpretentious clock tower with a humble bell. Here, again, the history of the city speaks through its buildings, for Palazzo Roncale, built by the Venetians' favoured architect, proclaims their victory over Ferrara, symbolized by Rossetti's Palazzo Roverella. With its quaint trapezoidal floor plan, Palazzo Roncale also displays Sanmicheli at his most impressive.

Venice was magnanimous to her new vassal, in 1584 granting

Rovigo the right to hold an annual fair. Initially this took place in August, around the Feast of the Assumption, but soon it was moved to October, in which month it is still celebrated today. In addition, Rovigo has its thrice-weekly market and the Lendinara fair, set up by the senate in 1665 and these days held from 8 to 11 September. The civic theatre, rebuilt in 1904 by the Milan architect Daniele Donghi, after a fire burned down its early nineteenth-century predecessor, hosts performances of Mozart, Puccini and Verdi.

Abutting on to the Piazza Vittorio Emanuele II is the city art gallery, the Pinacoteca del Accademia dei Concordi, built in 1814 by the local architect Sante Baseggio. The academy itself was founded in 1580, and in subsequent centuries collected over 600 paintings and a library of 180,000 volumes. In consequence, the Pinacoteca del Accademia is bursting with superb Venetian works of art, including portraits by Giambattista Tiepolo and paintings by Giovanni Bellini, Alessandro Longhi, Palma the Elder and Palma the Younger. On the briefest of visits, seek out Tiepolo's subtle portrait of a fur-clad, pensive Antonio Riccoboni, Giovanni Bellini's 'Madonna and Child' (with Mary in a delicious red robe planting a huge hand protectively on her infant son's chest) and his 'Christ carrying his Cross'. Among minor masters, I warmed to Sebastiano Mazzoni's seventeenth-century portrayal of the dying Cleopatra. As well as paintings and books (including a superb illuminated codex of Genesis and Ruth, created in the fourteenth century), the Pinacoteca houses a collection of local antiquities.

A new use for the barrel-vaulted monastery church of San Bartolomeo (which Rossetti rebuilt for the Olivetan order in 1480, and which boasts a baroque décor and a porticoed Renaissance cloister with tree ferns and a Sansovino-type well) is housing an overflow of the gallery's archaeological treasures from the province of Polesine. What these reveal is that Rovigo and the Polesine, whose river-watered plain has sustained a millennia of farmers, were inhabited by generations who traded in bronze and ceramics with the Etruscans, with the Aegean and with the Greeks.

From Piazza Vittorio Emanuele II, walk into the neighbouring Piazza Garibaldi (in which a bronze Garibaldi sternly sits astride a bronze charger) and then follow Via Silvestri to discover the Romanesque-Gothic church of Santi Francesco e Giustina, built in the fourteenth century and much restored in the nineteenth. It houses a fifteenth-century marble *pietà* by Tullio Lombardo and a 'Madonna with Saints' by Sebastiano Filippi (who was known as Il Bastiano), plus Girolamo da Carpi's quaint 'Manifestation of the Holy Spirit at the Last Supper'.

Behind its apse is Piazza XX Settembre, in which rises the church of the Beata Vergine del Soccorso, an octagon and thus better known as La Rotonda. The octagonal upper storey rises coolly from an octagonal portico. Francesco Zamberlano, a pupil of Palladio, designed the church in 1594. Its name derives from a miracle-working image of the Virgin Mary, frescoed in the sixteenth century and now gracing the church's altar. Henceforth this church was the focus of Rovigo's civic pride. La Rotonda is flanked by a six-storeyed campanile, which was commissioned from Baldassare Longhena in 1655 (though not finished until 1784), a campanile which makes not the slightest pretence to match the design of the church. Inside La Rotonda the citizens have covered the walls with paintings by such seventeenth-century Venetian baroque masters as Francesco Maffei, Andrea Celesti, Pietro Liberi, Pietro Muttoni and Antonio Zanchi. The gilded wooden altar was carved by Giovanni Caracchio, a native of Rovigo, in 1607.

Rovigo's baroque cathedral, dedicated to St Stephen and built in the eighteenth century by Vincenzo Bellettato, is less fascinating than La Rotonda, though its sixteenth-century bronze candelabrum (which may be by Sansovino) is impressive enough, and behind an altar in the left transept is a 'Resurrection' by Palma the Younger.

If you are game for visiting more excellent churches, then before leaving Rovigo find first of all Sant'Agostino, which was built in

1588; then the little thirteenth-century Chiesetta del Cristo (with a façade added in 1889 by Raffaele Cattaneo, an architect born in Rovigo), which houses a cell where it is said that St Francis of Assisi slept in 1231; next San Michele, built in the late sixteenth century for the Capuchins and sheltering a painting by Palma the Younger of St Francis receiving the stigmata; fourthly, the church of the Madonna dei Sabbioni, which dates back to the twelfth century, though it has been much restored, and boasts a couple of eighteenth-century statues by Sante Baseggio; and, finally, the sixteenth-century San Domenico, in which hangs a 'Madonna with Saints' painted by pupils of Titian.

Yet for centuries before the dominance of Rovigo, Adria – just over twenty kilometres to the east through the canal-channelled fields along the N443 – was the chief centre of this region. From Adria the Adriatic takes its name. On the way to the city, at Villadose on the right bank of the River Adigetto, you can arrange to visit in the mornings except on Sunday (telephone 0425-90046) the imposing Villa Patella, which was built at the end of the sixteenth century for the Counts Patella.

One reason for Adria's former pre-eminence is that in the Roman era the sea reached this town, only gradually retreating behind sand dunes over the centuries. Today Adria is situated on the basin of the Canal Bianco and possessed of an archaeological museum (at no. 1 Piazza Etruschi) with some very fine Roman and Etruscan remains, as well as a section devoted to the prehistoric settlements of the Po delta. The eighteenth-century church of Santa Maria Assunta della Tomba (which stands on the site of an eighth-century church) has an octagonal font dating from the eighth century as well as a depiction of the falling asleep of the Blessed Virgin Mary, done in terracotta in the fifteenth century and attributed to Michele da Firenze. The font is a Roman basin, with an eighth-century inscription. The cathedral of Adria, though radically restored in the nineteenth century, also reveals the antiquity of the town, for one of its columns carries a fifth-century

Coptic bas-relief depicting an enthroned Madonna, and the crypt has fading Byzantine frescos.

Continue east through Loreo to reach Rosolina on the N309, which runs north to Chioggia. Chioggia is an oddity, a mixture of fishermen, market gardeners, idlers, impatient motorists, haunters of cafés and two or three splendid relics of its former elegance. One of these is a bridge. The Ponte Vigo is built of marble and decorated with lions, which the Venetians (only half an hour away by boat or motor car) insult by calling them 'cats'. Resting on islands connected to the mainland by a couple of bridges, Chioggia juts out between the southern end of the Venetian lagoon and the Venetian gulf. The sixteenth-century Ponte Garibaldi leads to the cathedral, which was rebuilt in 1633 by Longhena, though it retains its fourteenth-century campanile. Inside, one of the paintings in the Cappella dei Santi Felice e Fortunato is an early work by Tiepolo. The pulpit of 1677 is by Cavalieri.

San Martino, next to the *duomo*, dates from 1392. Its belfry is octagonal; it houses a polyptych by Paolo Veronese. From here the handsome Corso del Popolo runs past palaces and churches, most of them eighteenth-century, to arrive at the church of San Andrea Apostolo, which has a Romanesque belfry and a baroque façade. Then turn right, cross over a couple of canals, and find San Domenico, to discover on the second altar on the right Vittore Carpaccio's last work, a painting of St Paul dated 1520. From Tintoretto the church has gained an 'Apparition of the Crucifix'; and finest of all, to my mind, is a 'Deposition' painted by Bassano.

This is a superb section of the Adriatic coast, with quays, courtyards and canals lined by low-lying fisherfolk's houses. While their womenfolk make lace, local fishermen still use lines, nets, eel-baskets and crab-pots to entrap the succulent inhabitants of the sea. Further out they catch tunny fish. They also cultivate mussels, and the stakes that hem these in are a noted feature of the seascape here. Fish are also reared in special farms (known as *valli*). Plentiful bream, red and grey mullet, sole and flounders swim in these waters. One romantic feature has recently disappeared, however. Fishermen of the Po delta used to sail in two-masted vessels with decorated sails. The masts and sails have now been supplanted by petrol and diesel motor engines.

Sottomarina, just east of Chioggia, has been developed as a major seaside resort, with six kilometres of broad sandy beaches, and hotels, *trattorias* and restaurants along its promenade looking out to sea. Between the mouths of the Rivers Adige and Brenta, Isola Verde is another bathing resort, with bungalows and apartments. And further south, between Chioggia and the Po delta, are the beaches of Rosolina Mare and the Isola di Albarella. The first has nine kilometres of often isolated sandy beach, beside which are cool pine woods. Here the Po delta is a haven for naturalists, particularly bird-watchers. One of Rosolina's chief products is the red, rose-shaped chicory, the *radicchio*, a staple ingredient in Venetan salads. And near to Isola di Albarella, the Po separates into hundreds of little watercourses. Its sediment has created small islands and embankments beside the coast. Apart from its 600 hectares of woodlands, lagoons and beaches, the island boasts tennis courts, two Olympic-size swimming pools, an 18-hole golf links and a harbour that can accommodate 500 pleasure boats. This resort also enterprisingly hosts music, ballet and film festivals.

Returning to Rovigo, a longer excursion would first run north to take in Monsélice, which sits at the foot of the Euganean hills (and etymologically means the 'silicate mountain'). As you approach Monsélice, the hills ahead resemble oversized molehills. Then a string of what look like pillboxes, climbing to a chapel and villa above a medieval defensive wall, give a foretaste of the pleasures to come. Monsélice is dominated by the partly ruined castle of Emperor Frederick II, with a galaxy of turrets and battlements and fortified rooms, which date from the eleventh to the sixteenth centuries and include a majestic fourteenth-century fireplace, polychrome wooden ceilings and a display of medieval and Renaissance arms and furniture.

For centuries Monsélice's strategic position, dominating the routes from the south to Padua and the Euganean hills, made it a coveted stronghold. In AD 602 the Lombards drove out the Byzantine rulers of the town. Next the lords of neighbouring Este took control, followed by the Ezzolino family. When Monsélice came under Carraresi rule, its fortifications were strengthened, as they were again by Frederick II. Under the protection of this imperial fortress, Ghibelline vassals lived peacefully in the surrounding plain. Only after 1405, when the city became a fief of Venice, did its strategic and military role decline.

The heart of the city is Piazza Mazzini, in which rises the Torre Civica, built in the thirteenth century and heightened in the next. Take the picturesque Via al Santuario to find, in succession, the *castello* and the Duomo Vecchio. The former is part thirteenth-, part fifteenth-century. Both the Duomo Vecchio and its campanile are Romanesque-Gothic constructions, exceedingly simple and harmonious. Find your way in through a gateway on the right-hand side to discover frescos painted by Venetian artists in the fifteenth century. Via al Santuario flanks the late-Renaissance Villa Nani, on whose walls sit sculpted dwarfs (*nani*). When the villa was enlarged in the eighteenth century it also gained the monumental baroque stairway climbing up its garden, which you can admire through huge double gates.

With extensive views over the adjoining plain, Via al Santuario continues as far as the Santuario delle Sette Chiese. (On this plain, incidentally, grow juicy peaches, which are known as *lorenzina*, since they ripen in August close to the feast of San Lorenzo.) The Santuario delle Sette Chiese is so named because the pillboxes turn out to be six separate chapels, designed by Scamozzi and decorated by Jacopo Negretti (who lived from 1544 to 1628 and is known as Palma the Younger), which lead up to the chapel of Villa Duodo. These curious buildings represent six miniature models of Roman churches. Their culmination, the chapel of San Giorgio, is a bizarre affair. Circular, it shelters behind its altar the skeleton of a Roman martyr, while other Roman martyrs lie in open cupboards, dressed up, but with their skulls peeping out. The altar is of *pietro duaro*, with an intarsia St George. By contrast, the villa itself, just beyond the chapel, is another of Vincenzo Scamozzi's fine legacies to the Veneto, built between 1593 and 1611, commissioned by a nobleman named Francesco Duodo. Stately, statued and splendid, with eighteenth-century modifications by Andrea Tirali, the villa now belongs to Padua university, which (alas) means that the ordinary traveller cannot get inside.

Two villas in the environs of Monsélice can be visited if you telephone in advance. The finest, set beside the Battaglia canal, is Villa Pisani (telephone 0429-74344). Attributed to Palladio, it was built for Francesco Pisani and frescoed in the 1560s, probably by Lattanzio Gambara. Villa Maldura Emo Capodilista (telephone 0429-77287), built in 1588 in the Palladian style, makes up for being less fine than Villa Pisani by boasting an attractive garden.

Another ruined castle guards Este, nine kilometres west of Monsélice and a centre renowned for its ceramics. You approach it by way of a plain that skirts the Euganean hills, with vineyards gently rising on the right. This is another of those towns in the Veneto beloved of Byron and Shelley. In 1817 and 1818 they stayed in Villa Kunkler, formerly a sixteenth-century Capuchin convent, with Byron's daughter Allegra.

Este is also ancient – as archaeological finds have revealed – frequented in earlier times by the Etruscans and the Celts. Its name derives from the old version of the River Adige, the Athestis, which washed its walls until a disastrous flood changed its course in 589. In the Middle Ages Este gave its name to one of the most powerful families of the region, the Estensi. After the Estensi had abandoned the city in 1275 to make their home at Ferrara, Este was disputed by the major families of this region – the Scaligers, the Visconti and the Carraresi. And approaching from Monsélice, you first come upon the surviving battlemented walls of the early fourteenth-century Castello Carrarese. Umbertino of

Carrara rebuilt it in 1340, and the fortress was once defended by a wall 1,000 metres long, guarded by fourteen towers, of which twelve still exist.

In front of them a Saturday market sets itself up from 06.00 to 14.00. Inside the walls stands Palazzo Mocenigo, a feudal stronghold transformed by the Mocenigo family, who acquired it in 1405. Most of what you see today dates from the late sixteenth century, and in one wing is one of Italy's finest archaeological collections, the Museo Nazionale Atestino. The curtain walls also enclose a flowery and extensive public garden.

Soon you reach the bridge over the river, with its baroque clock tower of 1690, near which is located the little classical church of San Rocco. The abbey-church of Este is dedicated to St Tecla and houses a fifteenth-century pulpit and a painting of 1759 by Giambattista Tiepolo depicting the saint interceding for the town during a plague in 1630. Rebuilt in 1708 by Antonio Gaspari, after an earthquake of 1688 had destroyed the previous church, St Tecla, which remains unfinished, stands on the site of a pagan temple to the river god Athestis.

Gaspari produced an elegant new design for the church – elliptical, and surrounded by chapels. Inside is a sixteenth-century crucifix, and a silver urn containing the earthly remains of Beatrice the Blessed. But a much more charming building, to my mind, is the twelfth-century Romanesque church of San Martino in Via P. Umberto, its belfry added in 1293 and today slightly leaning. And two other churches have fine paintings: a Byzantine icon, attributed to no less a person than St Luke himself, and a sixteenth-century 'Christ Crucified' by Gian Battista Maganza in the fifteenth-century Santa Maria delle Grazie; and a collection of paintings by the local artist Antonio Zanchi in the church of the Beata Vergine della Salute (which is known as the Madonna de Fuora and has two bell-towers).

Santa Maria delle Consolazione, built in 1505 (with a campanile of 1598), encompasses a Roman mosaic pavement and once contained a 'Madonna and Child' painted by Cima da Conegliano in 1504, until the authorities transported it to Este's Museo Nazionale Atestino. This painting alone makes a visit to the museum worthwhile. The artist has painted a musing Virgin, wearing a blood-red robe, a white mantle and a blue cloak lined with gold. Her infant, in a white corset, fondles his mother's neck. Behind the green curtain you glimpse a rocky Paduan countryside.

Guided tours of the huge Villa Pesara (telephone 0429-2101) at Este reveal a villa begun by Baldassare Longhena around 1670 and frescoed between 1760 and 1790 by Giovanni Scagliaro. Villa Miari De' Cumani, which you can visit daily in the afternoons (except on Mondays) from March to November, was built in the early seventeenth century (save for its nineteenth-century tower) and is surrounded by a romantic park designed by Osvaldo Paoletti in the 1870s. And on the way north to Calaone stands Villa Contarini (telephone 0429-2133), a late sixteenth-century country house, decorated in the early 1800s and dubbed 'Del Principe' after Alvise Contarini, who lived here and was doge of Venice between 1676 and 1684.

Leave the arcaded streets and squares of Este by way of the Rocca di Ponte Torre, undoubtedly the finest surviving stronghold of those built in the Middle Ages against marauders. Montagnana lies thirty-one kilometres further west along the N10. You have now entered the utterly flat countryside that will characterize the rest of this little tour, with cultivated fields, orchards and vineyards. Montagnana, a small city of much character, is still protected by superb medieval walls, stretching for 1,925 metres, dating from the thirteenth and fourteenth centuries and made of brick, limestone and trachyte. You can walk along them. They were begun on the orders of Ezzolino da Romana, who had conquered the city in 1242, and were completed under the Carraresi.

Of Montagnana's four fortified gates, two are magnificent: the thirteenth-century Porta Padova, with the Torre Ezzelina, and the Rocca degli Alberi (the fortress of the trees), which was built in

1388 where a triple-arched bridge crosses the moat, is thirty-two metres in height, has a keep and little barbican to guard it and also carries a double drawbridge. The Porta Vicenza was transformed into a bell tower in the sixteenth century, while the Porta XX Settembre dates from the nineteenth century. Plane trees encircle Montagnana's wide moat, while twenty-four polygonal towers, seventy-five metres apart, protect the rest of the walls. And these ramparts provide a perfect venue for the annual *palio* contest, between the quarters of the city and ten neighbouring localities, which is held here at the beginning of August. The contest is a revival of the festivities in which the people indulged during the Middle Ages to mark the departure of the Ezzolini tyrants.

Francesco Pisani, whose villa you have already seen at Monsélice, in 1553 commissioned Palladio to design Palazzo Pisani (telephone 0429-81368) near the Porta Padova. It has a double-storeyed portico, and Alessandro Vittoria supplied its statues of the four seasons in the 1570s and the winged victory on the façade. Sansovino provided the sixteenth-century portal of Montagnana's massive Gothic cathedral (begun in 1431, completed in 1502), which is built of brick and stands in the irregular, arcaded Piazza Vittorio Emanuele. Over the marble portal and the carved doors are sculpted the symbols of the four evangelists. The cathedral's tunnel-vaulted interior is a treat, with a 'Transfiguration' painted in 1555 by Veronese for Sansovino's high altar, stalls of 1555 and frescos painted in the fifteenth and sixteenth centuries (some of them by G. Buonconsiglio). Another fresco, by Aliense, celebrates the Battle of Lepanto, when in 1571 the Venetian and Spanish fleets destroyed that of the Turks in the Mediterranean.

Each Thursday the piazza welcomes a morning market. Here, among eighteenth-century houses, stands a pawnshop of 1497, and the Casa di Risparmo in this square is part of a pastiche of a medieval palace, with a pulpit-balcony on the corner and a green and red frieze. It also houses the tourist office. Over the roofs of the houses rises the fifteenth-century brick campanile of the fourteenth- and fifteenth-century church of San Francesco. To explore this church more closely, turn into Via Carrarese beside the pastiche *palazzo* and then right into Via Cesare Battista. Here is the Municipio, the mid-sixteenth-century work of Sanmicheli, though enlarged in the subsequent two centuries. At the end of Via Cesare Battista turn right and walk along the inside of the city walls to find San Francesco, in which is a canvas by Palma the Younger.

Drive on to Legnago, on the way to which you pass through Bevilacqua with its superb medieval castle. Legnago nestles on the left bank of the River Adige and is the home of the Fioroni museum, a collection of weapons and medieval tools, Renaissance ceramics and mementoes of the Risorgimento and the Second World War. Almost the sole reminder of Legnago's once important role as part of Austria's southern defences is the ruined Torrione in Piazza della Libertà. And a short way due west, at Cerea, stands Villa Tacoli Dionisi, designed by a retired seafarer and soldier in the 1740s (see p.45).

The road back to Rovigo from Legnago runs for forty-five kilometres along the fertile valley lying between the Po and the Adige. Halfway there, on the banks of the Adigetto, Badia Polésine boasts a former abbey, the Abbazia la Vangadizza, founded in the tenth century, though what remains dates chiefy from the fifteenth century (and Napoleon destroyed some of this when he suppressed the abbey in 1810). In the Middle Ages this abbey had become powerful enough to emancipate itself from the control of the local bishop, becoming subordinate only to the Pope himself. Successive abbots presided over land reclamation in the Po delta, meanwhile furthering scholarship and education in the region. They also enhanced their monastic church. Its frescos were painted in the sixteenth century, its campanile was built in the twelfth century (and wears a kind of dunce's cap), and the chapel of the Madonna was added in 1490. The cloister of 1233, with its octagonal stone pillars and stone arches, has a fifteenth-century well and a loggia, and gives way to a refectory of 1466. In the Middle Ages this abbey made Badia Polésine the most important cultural centre in the Polesine until the rise of Rovigo. Another fifteenth-century building here is the Gothic Palazzo degli Estensi, built by the masters of the whole region.

This little spot has more lovely palaces, some of them washed by the river: the fifteenth-century Palazzo Rossini (today the home of the Banca Cattolica del Veneto), the seventeenth-century Palazzo Baccaglini and the eighteenth-century Palazzo Tappari, which is contemporary with the parish church. The oratory of Madonna della Salute was begun in the seventeenth century and finished in the next, and Badia Polésine built its lavishly decorated civic theatre in 1813. Apart from its abbey, other churches include San Giovanni in Piazza Vittorio Emanuele II, which houses a fifteenth-century 'Ecce Homo' by Pietro Lombardo. This church was built in 1761 on the remains of an earlier house of God of 1123, and its façade is ornamented with statues of Saints Joseph, John the Baptist and Theobald. Since Theobald is also patron saint of Badia Polésine, his mortal remains can be inspected inside the church in an altar sculpted in eighteenth-century marble by Giuseppe Fadiga. As well as these delights, Badia Polésine has a civic museum (the Museo Baruffaldi), which presents the history of the city from the Middle Ages until the Second World War.

Nine kilometres nearer Rovigo you reach Lendinara. On the way, at Salvaterra, look out for Villa Pellegrini (telephone 0425-51745), its central building and two side loggias built in the early seventeenth century, stuccoed in the eighteenth and frescoed with mythological scenes by Andrea Urbani in the early 1770s.

Lendinara was the home of the Canozi, a celebrated family of Renaissance woodcarvers. To gauge their skills, visit the Palazzo Communale, which preserves a fifteenth-century carved grille by Lorenzo Canozio, whom Piero della Francesca once declared 'as dear to me as a brother'. The city boasts Renaissance and baroque palaces, including the striking Palazzo Dolfin-Marchiori by Vincenzo Scamozzi. Its eighteenth-century sanctuary of the

Madonna del Pilastrello has an altarpiece by Veronese depicting the Ascension, as well as paintings by such masters as Il Guercino and Spagnoletto. The Cappella del Bagno of this church dates from an earlier sixteenth-century building by Giacomo Baccari and derives its name from a font that contains water reputedly able to heal the sick. A further prophylactic against illness is the presence here of a renowned statue of the Black Virgin, discovered in an olive grove in 1509.

For me, more entrancing than these are the tombs of an Englishwoman, Jessie White, and her husband, Garibaldi's lieutenant Alberto Morio. As Garibaldi liberated Italy, she was his Florence Nightingale, though she had no staff of trained nurses. 'Fanatical in her republicanism, lacking in toleration and charm of manner, she had the spartan virtues of her creed and a power of complete self-sacrifice which she had learnt perhaps from her friend and master, Mazzini,' wrote George Macaulay Trevelyan in his *Garibaldi and the Making of Italy*. Garibaldi, he added, knew well how much he owed to Jessie and how many of his best followers were saved by her ceaseless exertions.

Superficially at least there was little in common between this lady of fixed and fiery faith and the comfortable citizens of her native island. But they were ready to praise her when they heard how she attended the wretched pallets of hundreds of wounded Italians, who blessed her in their pain and her country for her sake.

Once a boy of twelve suffered an amputation while sitting in Jessie's lap. She wept, she confessed, more than he did.

Another handsome house of God here is the cathedral of Santa Sofia, which was decorated in the eighteenth century and has a campanile built in 1797 by Francesco Antonio Baccari. At ninety metres, this rates (after the campanile of Venice) as the second highest in the Veneto. One of the treasures of the cathedral, Domenico Mancini's 'Madonna with an angel musician', was painted in 1511 and is kept in the sacristy. San Biagio is a classical church, rebuilt in the eighteenth century by Baccari but preserving its portal of 1531 and a 'Visitation' painted in 1525 by Sebastiano Filippi da Lendinara.

Before returning to Rovigo from Lendinara, make a diversion south-east to Fratta Polésine, for this is villa country, and here are three in particular that are well worth seeing: Villa Bragadin, which is modelled on Palladio's work; the square Villa Avezzú Pignatelli (telephone 0425-68129, though visits are restricted to Saturday afternoons); and, above all, Villa Badoer, which was built by Palladio himself in the 1550s and can be visited at any time. All are not only exceedingly fine but also quite different in feeling. The first is cubic, in colour pale yellow picked out in white. Villa Avezzú Pignatelli has a simple, neat portico and was in part decorated by Palladio's contemporary Giallo Fiorentino. The third is the most celebrated villa in the province of Rovigo.

Raised on a stone platform, Villa Badoer boasts an entrance modelled on Greek Doric temples and is flanked by curving Greek colonnades. Antique statues stand on basins in its garden. Its interior was frescoed by the mannerist Giallo Fiorentino with scenes of gods, nymphs and youths on horseback. The paint, alas, was pitted and flaking when last I saw it. But the authentic Palladian touch is still visible in the architecture. 'The cornice, like a crown, encompasses the whole house,' glowed the master. 'The frontispiece, over the loggias, forms a beautiful sight, because it makes the middle part higher than the sides. Lower on the plane are found the places for the steward, bailiff or farmer, stables and other suitable for a villa.'

Excavations at Fratta Polésine in 1974 and at Narde in 1987 revealed that this region was inhabited in the eleventh century BC, and the former chapel of Villa Labia at Fratta Polésine has been turned into a small museum recording this. Four main waterways – the Po and the Adige (the two longest rivers in Italy), the Adigetto and the Tartaro-Canal Bianco – cross this region, which undulates gently as a result of centuries of reclamation. A network of canals and drainage ditches subdivides the delta (known as Il Polésine) still further. The region is dotted with isolated farms and their courtyards, as well as with the white manor houses, often with a large round fireplace, that served as homes for the wardens of the delta. Canals and locks, broad farmlands, wells, reed beds, willows and groves of poplars enliven the scenery. *Grisoleri*, that is, men who cut reeds for fences, work in special plantations. In autumn they leave their homes to look after sportsmen and -women who conceal themselves in oak barrels in order to shoot ducks, of which there are countless varieties (among them garganey, wigeon, merganser and smew).

This estuary is extraordinarily complicated. In recorded history the Po burst its banks in 1152 and forced its way to the Adriatic by way of three branches. Then it broke up into six streams: from south to north, the Po di Goro (on the boundary with the province of Ferrara), the Po di Gnocca, the Po di Tolle, the Po di Pila (which itself diverges into the estuaries of the Tramontana and the Scirocco), the Po di Maistra and the Po di Levante. Its dunes, swamps and marshes provide year-round sanctuary for sand martins, grey partridges, avocets, cormorants, great-crested grebes and little grebes, coots, snipe, marsh harriers, black-tailed godwits, woodcock, lapwings, little egrets, grey herons, moorhens, pochards, sedge warblers, bittern, teal, reed buntings, every kind of warbler, crakes and mallard. Migrating visitors include purple herons, wild geese, pochards and pintails. Animals too find refuge here: moles, hares, polecats, hedgehogs, shrews, weasels and otters.

Il Polésine encompasses such unspoilt spots as Ceneselli, Castelmassa and Bergantino, on the way west towards Verona. But *cognoscenti* of Venetan villas will above all make their way south from Rovigo to Polesella on the River Po (which forms the southern boundary of the Veneto), for here are no fewer than four exquisite ones. Villa Morosini Mantovani (telephone 049-701482) was built in the late seventeenth century for Francesco Morosini, doge of Venice from 1688 to 1694, who was nicknamed the Peloponnesian. Villa Armellini (telephone 0425-361363), a three-storeyed house with two balconies built at the end of the seventeenth century, is known as the villa of the seven heads because of the crazy, grotesque masks that adorn its entrance and windows. Inside is an oval portrait of Doge Francesco, along with biblical scenes painted by Mattia Bortoloni in the early eighteenth century. The three-storeyed Villa Selmi Serafini (telephone 049-651459) was built in the sixteenth century, much altered in the late eighteenth (when it gained its delicately decorated doors) and is surrounded by a romantic park. And the three-storeyed Villa Rosetta Chiereghin (telephone 0425-94161), with its powerfully arched loggia, dates from the late seventeenth century, has a little chapel, and its baroque interior, probably the work of Andrea Brustolon, is decorated in pink and grey marble.

Padua, the Brenta and the Euganean hills

Around two sides of old Padua flows the River Bacchiglione, protecting the city, a defence reinforced by ancient walls. And in Padua's surviving architecture you can read much of the city's history. A colony of Rome in 89 BC, and a Municipium forty years later, Padua's Roman past is revealed in the ruins of its amphitheatre and forum, in traces of the harbour and the bridges the Romans built over the river they called the Medoacus, and above all in the pattern of the city streets, laid out – like so many we have seen in this region – along the former Roman *Cardus* and *Decumanus*.

In the early Christian era the city developed into a major Christian centre and was the seat of a bishop from the fourth century onwards. Again, there are visible remains of this epoch, in the church of Santa Giustina, whose chapel of the Madonna dates from the fifth century. An attack by barbarians in 602 destroyed much of the city, but Padua rose again and, ringed by a new set of Romanesque walls, began rebuilding. The new Santa Giustina (though much enlarged and enhanced in later centuries) dates from this rebirth, as does Santa Sofia, which was begun at the end of the ninth century and finished by the twelfth. Today Santa Sofia is the oldest church in the city, rising in the north-east, with its sturdy Romanesque tower and its brick Romanesque apse, which gives a deceptive air of simplicity.

Soon the Paduans wanted secular palaces worthy of their city's status, an ambition accomplished first of all by the Palazzo della Ragione of 1215 to 1219 and next by the Palazzo degli Anziani of 1285. These still remain at the civic heart of the city, joined by the Palazzo della Cancelleria.

Two splendid churches dominate the southernmost part of Padua. Above the most southerly, the Benedictine Santa Giustina, rise eight cupolas. Il Riccio designed this pale pink, brick church in 1501, and during the next thirty years Andrea Moroni built it. A couple of griffins flank the steps to its entrance. The west façade was, alas, never faced with the intended stone and marble, and the interior, though massively baroque, is disappointingly bare.

Its cruciform shape houses baroque altars with fantastic figures and marquetry choir stalls of 1566, made by a Norman who was renamed Riccardo Turigny by the Italians. For this church Veronese painted a 'Martyrdom of St Justine' in 1575. Look out for remains of the older church (to the right of the choir): the chapel of the Virgin, dating from the fifth century and housing the relics of St Prosdocimus, the first bishop of Padua; a thirteenth-century Romanesque doorway; a fourteenth-century chapel; and a fifteenth-century choir with yet more fine inlaid stalls, these made in 1477. The Benedictine monastery dates from the fifteenth and sixteenth centuries.

Outside the church is the elliptical Prato della Valle, a garden with plane trees surrounded by a canal (which, alas, is itself often surrounded by intrusive parked cars). Its shape derives from the former Roman circus. The four baroque bridges crossing its waters bear obelisks and urns, and the garden is bordered by eighty-seven eighteenth-century statues of illustrious Paduans.

Halfway up the east side of the Prato, take Via Briusco (named after an architect who lived from 1471 to 1532) and then Via

Donatello to reach a much quieter spot: the oldest botanical garden in Europe. When Goethe visited Padua in 1786 he grew extremely cheerful here, considering as he did that botany was a subject of profound and far-reaching consequences. Here, in fact, he finally accepted a theory of evolution. But anyone who adores gardens (I cultivate two of my own) will relish this one. In summer you can walk round it from 09.00 to 17.00, though in winter and on holidays the gates close at 13.00. Still sheltered by its sixteenth-century circular wall (with eighteenth-century statues and busts), the botanical garden was founded in 1545 to serve the apothecaries of the university medical school. In the fashion of many Renaissance gardens, axial paths meeting at the centre divide the land into quarters, which hold stone-edged triangular beds. Padua's closeness to sea-faring Venice meant that numerous exotic plants arrived here, and in 1565 her botanical garden was the first in Europe to grow lilac, as well as being the first, in 1590, to grow the potato.

From here you can see the spires and domes of the basilica of Sant'Antonio, which rises to the north of the Orto Botanico in the Piazza del Santo. 'Il Santo' is what the Paduans call the basilica of Sant'Antonio. In this piazza stands a superb bronze, the equestrian statue of Erasmo da Narni (known as Il Gattamelata), which was commissioned by his family from Donatello after the Venetian *condottiere*'s death in 1443. Finished ten years later, it depicts Erasmo as an old man, yet still fired with the same fury as his magnificent horse. The steed seems to have no neck, and its flamboyant tail is tied in a bow.

Sant'Antonio was built to house the bones of a milder hero, St Antony of Padua, who was in fact born in Lisbon in 1195 and died just outside Padua at Arcella in 1231. The son of a noble family, he entered the Lisbon monastery of the Canons Regular of São Vivente. Within two years Antony's questing spirit longed to devote itself more passionately to the service of his faith and, inspired by the tales of the first Franciscan martyrs in Morocco, he managed to be sent there.

106

Illness forced his return, and when the ship carrying the saint back to Europe was blown off course, he landed in Sicily. There he joined the Franciscans, was ordained and, as his preaching fame grew, was sent to northern Italy and southern France in the hope that he would convert heretics. The year 1221 found him preaching daily throughout Lent in Padua, attacking avarice and usury in the open air, for the crowds flocking to hear him were too great to cram into the churches. Two years later St Francis of Assisi made Antony the first professor of theology for his friars. Working ceaselessly, Antony ruined his already precarious health, and on 13 June 1231 he died aged only thirty-six.

Pope Gregory IX canonized Antony within a year of his death, and the Paduans began building his basilica immediately. His reputation for helping others multiplied after his death. He became the patron of miners and of lovers, of women in childbirth and of the poor. In his lifetime a fellow-monk had borrowed Antony's psalter without permission, returning it in fear after seeing a frightful apparition, and in consequence after his death Antony developed a reputation for helping people find their lost property. Oddly enough, this charitable man is venerated as an admiral both by the Portuguese (who attributed their victory over the French in 1710 to his aid) and by the Spanish (who believed he helped them expel the Moors from Oran in 1733).

The basilica in Padua where his remains still lie was specifically designed to enable worshippers to venerate the saint, and crowds of them still do so. Although its façade is Romanesque and its two slender octagonal campaniles Gothic, its spirit seems initially entirely Byzantine, with six spherical domes and a conical central cupola.

Inside, the basilica transforms itself into a Gothic church, cruciform in style and 115 metres long. At the east end is a delicate, richly decorated apse, with an ambulatory to allow pilgrims to walk round in an orderly fashion. The place is filled with architectural and sculptural gems. Tullio Lombardo sculpted

the statue of St John the Baptist on one font; Tiziano Aspetti
the statue of Jesus on another. Gattamelata, whose equestrian
statue you have seen outside, lies in a tomb of 1443 designed by
Bellano; his son Gianantonio lies in another of 1455 by Pietro
Lombardo.

St Antony himself lies in his own chapel in the left transept.
Il Riccio designed this chapel in 1500, Giovanni and Andreolo
de' Santi built it and Gian Maria Falconetto created its stuccoed
ceiling, which is picked out in gold. The saint's shrine stands
behind an altar made by Aspetti in 1593. Among its bas-reliefs
are two superb ones by Sansovino. They depict Antony raising
to life, first, a young girl who had fallen into a well (the face of
the girl's grandmother is masterly) and, second, the son of her
sister, also raised to life after he had been drowned for three
days. The other two reliefs, done by Tullio Lombardo in 1525,
do not match Sansovino's in skill, their perspective being less
sure; but they overreach his in savagery, especially the scene in
which a dead man's chest is slashed.

Ignoring these, most of the faithful wish simply to touch the
shrine of Antony, just as Joseph Addison watched them do nearly
300 years ago. As a Protestant, Addison slightly looked down
on their faith. Here, he wrote:

Good Catholics rub their beads, and smell Antony's bones, which they
say have in them a natural perfume, though very like apoplectic balm;
and what would make one suspect they [the clergy of the basilica]
rub the marble with it, it is observed that the scent is stronger in the
morning than at night.

Whatever the cause, this perfume no longer rises from Antony's
sacred bones.

Further on, in the left transept, is a chapel created in the
1370s by Andreolo and Giovanni de' Santi. It was decorated in
the same century by Altachiero da Zeno with frescos depicting
the crucifixion of Jesus, stories of the Madonna and the legends
of St James the Great. The last are extraordinarily vivid. St James

is depicted asleep, on his way to Santiago de Compostela (various representations of the saint growing smaller as he gets further away) and, in the most vivid scene of all, saved from a falling wall by the heavenly succour of Jesus. Almost as dramatic is the Battle of Clavigo, the legendary conflict of 844 when the saint is said to have appeared on the side of the Spanish King Ramiro I in order to slay countless Moors.

But the finest work of art in the whole basilica is the high altar. Its choir is guarded by mid-seventeenth-century bronze doors, while the walls are enhanced by bronze reliefs of scenes from the Old Testament by Il Riccio and Bartolomeo Bellano. The high altar itself, sculpted by Donatello and his pupils between 1445 and 1450, when Donatello was almost sixty, was scarcely appreciated for centuries. Many of its bronzes were dispersed, being reassembled only in 1895. Among the masterpieces are a crucifix, flanked by the six patron saints of Padua (Saints Prosdocimus, Daniel, Antony, Francis of Assisi, Giustina and Louis of Anjou) and the Madonna in her glory. The stone 'Deposition' is also the work of Donatello, while the splendid bronze candelabrum was made by Il Riccio in 1515.

A baroque chapel serves worshippers in the ambulatory. The triple cloisters, which you enter from the north side of the church, date from the thirteenth to the fifteenth centuries. In the middle of the first grows a huge majolica tree. In the second is a well, and on the wall is a monument to the composer Giuseppe Tartini, who was born in 1692 and renounced his vocation as a clergyman in order to write music. He married the niece of the Archbishop of Padua without permission and was obliged to flee the city, but was forgiven and came back in 1728. Tartini had another forty-two years to live, and spent most of them composing string music that is said to be devilishly hard to play. His most famous work is appropriately called the *Trillo del Diavolo*.

The third cloister has another fine majolica tree, and from here you leave Sant'Antonio. Once again outside the basilica, do not miss the fourteenth-century oratory of San Giorgio, on the left of the great church, which was founded as the memorial chapel of Raimondo Lupi in 1377. The following year Altachiero da Zeno and Jacopo Avanzo (who were pupils of Giotto) began to fresco the chapel. Beside the oratory rises the Scuola di San Antonio. Here are more frescos, three of them painted by the young Titian in 1512, glowing with his characteristic colours and displaying his mastery at painting the Venetan countryside. Among their treats is a scene where Antony re-attaches the severed foot of a young man, and another in which a jealous husband stabs his innocent wife.

Cross from Gattamelata's statue to the arcaded, shady Via del Santo, with its bars, shops and *trattorias* (among whose Paduan specialities is chicken with beaten whites of eggs, while the best wine comes from the vineyards you shall shortly see in the Euganean hills). To the north Via Umberto I leads to a thirteenth-century palace, with battlements, a Roman-esque doorway, a balcony and towers, and to a Lombardic house, the Casa Olzignani, whose fanciful windows and arcade crumble a little. Ponte delle Torricelle now crosses the river into Via Roma, on the left of which rise the arcades of the late fourteenth-century Gothic church of Santa Maria dei Servi. Its porch dates from the sixteenth century and inside are frescos, among them a *Pietà* by Jacopo da Montagnana and Renaissance sculptures. One ought to regard these as masterpieces, but after the two churches you have just visited one can even feel let down.

Via Roma continues north past the university to the secular heart of Padua, just off Piazza Cavour, where stands the most celebrated café in the Veneto. Long the haunt of intellectuals, politicians and students, who helped to foment the insurrection against Austria of 8 February 1848, the neo-classical Caffé Pedrocchi was modelled in 1831 on the Acropolis by its architect, Giuseppe Japelli (1783–1852). It is an extremely inept copy. Named after its first owner, Antonio Pedrocchi, the café is a remarkable concoction inside of white, red and green salons, separated by

Ionic columns, while on the first floor is a 'philharmonic room' dedicated to Rossini.

Walk back to Padua's university, founded in 1222 and thus one of the oldest in Europe. The building you see today dates from the sixteenth century, and incorporates the oldest anatomical theatre in the world, built by a surgeon named Fabrizio d'Acquapendente in 1594. Long before that time Padua university had welcomed Dante, Thomas Linacre and Petrarch as students. Galileo held the chair of mathematics here, and you can still see the seat (or *cattedra*) from which he taught between the years 1592 and 1610 (when the Grand-Duke of Tuscany summoned him to Florence). During those seminal years he invented first a kind of thermometer, next a proportional compass and, third, a refracting telescope. He also made the astronomical discoveries that were to lead to his downfall, ascertaining that the Milky Way was a series of innumerable stars, sighting the four satellites of Jupiter and noting the spots on the sun (which led him to the conclusive proof that the Copernican system of astronomy was correct and the Aristotelian system erroneous).

The tower of 1572 is contemporary with the bulk of the main university building, although the façade was added in 1757. Andrea Moroni designed the armorial-encrusted courtyard in 1552, and the statue at the foot of the stairs represents a pioneering feminist, Elena Cornaro Piscopia, who in the late seventeenth century became the first woman to be awarded a doctorate here.

Moroni also designed the Municipio on the other side of the street, though today it has a façade added in the late 1930s. Moroni embodied in his building an earlier thirteenth-century tower, which had belonged to the palace of the medieval Podestàs of Padua. The Paduans seem never to have stopped rebuilding their finest creations, and opposite rises another example of this habit, the massive brick and stone Palazzo della Ragione, dating originally from 1219 but rebuilt in 1306 by the architect-monk Fra Giovanni degli Eremitani. To him is due the wood and lead roof that resembles a huge, upturned keel.

Paduans have dubbed this palace 'Il Salone', from the huge interior hall, which measures over seventy-eight metres in length and is also twenty-eight metres wide and twenty-seven metres high. You visit it through a courtyard opposite the Municipio and up a noble flight of steps. Once the ceiling carried frescos by Giotto depicting astrological signs and planets, but a fire destroyed these in 1420. Niccolò Miretto was commissioned to redecorate the salon, and his religious and astrological scenes, which now cover the walls and vault, may well have been inspired by Giotto's originals.

As for the wooden horse that inhabits this great hall, it is a copy of one that Donatello created for a festival in 1466. Like Gattamelata's horse, it has a tail tied with a bow; it also has a better neck. Here Donatello was supposedly re-creating the Trojan horse, for legend (repeated by the Roman historian Livy, who was born just outside Padua) has it that the city was founded by a Trojan named Antenor, the brother of Priam. Another curiosity in this room is a block of stone, the *Pietra del Vituperio*, on which unfortunate debtors were once required to perch.

Via del Municipio leads from the left of this *palazzo* through an archway into the arcaded Piazza delle Erbe, from where you gain a fine view of 'Il Salone'. Living up to the name of the piazza in which it stands, the palace houses on its ground floor a market, which spills over into the neighbouring streets as well as into the Piazza della Frutta,on the other side.

A short series of cobbled and arcaded streets lead west to reach the Piazza del Duomo. Loosely based on a plan of Michelangelo, the cathedral was built in 1552 by Andrea da Valle and Agostino Righetto. On its site a cathedral had stood since the sixth century. The façade is raw and unfinished, the interior grand and spacious, housing tombs dating from the fourteenth to the sixteenth centuries. Much more charming is the thirteenth-century baptistry, which rises to the right of the *duomo*. Square, with a cupola, its interior was covered in frescos around 1380 by the Florentine Giusto de' Menabuioi. A double frieze depicts scenes from Genesis. The four evangelists appear in the pendentives. The lives of Jesus and John the Baptist fill more spaces; the apse has scenes from the Apocalypse; and the Virgin in her glory occupies pride of place over the door.

An impressive Renaissance palace shades the north side of the cathedral piazza, a building with massive pillars and arcades. Its architect was Gian Maria Falconetto, who in 1531 remodelled an existing palace on this spot. The arcade was frescoed by G. B. Bissono, Domenico Campagnola and G. Gione. Beyond it and beyond the Palazzo del Monte di Pietà of 1520 is the homely Piazza dei Signori, where you can see a fourteenth-century portico surviving from the Carraresi palace, which the Palazzo del Capitanio replaced at the beginning of the seventeenth century. In this piazza the lion of St Mark growls down from a column dating from the first century AD. This column was once part of the portico of Padua's profitable wool market.

The southern side of the square is shaded by the marble-clad Gran Guardia (whose proper name is the Loggia del Consiglio dei Nobili), begun by Annibale Maggi da Bassano in the Lombardic style in 1496 and finished off by a portico added by Biagio Bigoio in 1523. Enlivening the western side of the square is the Palazzo del Capitanio, built in 1605 for the Venetian rulers of Padua. Most of them belonged to the Carraresi family and, as we have noted, this palace replaced their much older castle.

In 1532 Falconetto added a triumphal Ionic arch-tower to the palace, in order to incorporate the oldest astrological clock in Italy. As well as signalling the twenty-four hours of the day, this clock, built in 1343 by Giovanni Caldiero to the specifications of two mathematicians (Jacopo and Giovanni Dondi), also displays the passage of the constellations and planets. A little square beyond this triumphal arch, known as the Piazza al Corte Capitaniato, is bordered by sixteenth-century houses and also by the Liviano, built by Gio Ponti in 1939 and serving as the university arts faculty and also as a museum of art and archaeology. It opens only on Saturdays, but is well worth seeking out, especially for the works of Bartolommeo Ammanati, a wax model by Donatello and, among its Greek and Roman sculptures, an Athena of the fourth century BC.

Via San Clemente leads past a deconsecrated and abandoned church into Piazza della Frutta, where you can admire yet another side of the Palazzo Ragione. Here stand two more ancient palaces: the fragmentary Palazzo Consiglio, which was built in 1283, and the Palazzo degli Anziani, but two years younger. The narrow, arcaded and sweet Via Boccalerie runs north to Via Santa Lucia and the baroque church of Santa Lucia, with its riotous statues and its grisaille frescos by Tiepolo and Ceruti. Beside it stands the Renaissance Scuola di San Rocco, built between 1480 and 1525. Its frescos are superb, mostly by Domenico Campagnola and Girolamo del Santo and devoted to the life of St Roch.

The Scuola di San Rocco rises on the southern side of Piazza Insurrezione. Although Padua is now becoming modern, this quarter still retains a fine handful of older buildings, in particular those in Via Santa Lucia to the east of the church of the same name. Here stands above all the twelfth-century Casa di Ezzelino, on the corner of Via Marsilio da Padova.

In Piazza Garibaldi at the end of Via Santa Lucia is a thirteenth-century gateway, once part of the city wall. Known as the Porta Altinate, it opens into Via Altinate, at the end of which stands the church of Santa Sofia.

Walk from Piazza Garibaldi north along Corso Garibaldi to find on the right the church of the Eremitani. The Romanesque-Gothic building, constructed between 1276 and 1306 as part of an Augustinian monastery, was almost completely destroyed by the bombs of 1944. Although it has been faithfully rebuilt, nothing can replace the chapel that Andrea Mantegna (born on an island between Padua and Vicenza in 1431) frescoed in his early twenties. But much still delights. The Renaissance façade has bas-reliefs depicting the occupations of the months and sculpted by the Florentine Niccolò Baroncelli in the 1440s. Inside among the impressive tombs is one on the left designed in the fourteenth century by Andreolo da Venezia for Jacopo da Carrara and inscribed with a Latin epitaph by Petrarch. On the right is another of the same era, this one housing the dust of Umbertino da Carrara. Bartolommeo Ammanati designed a more flamboyant mausoleum in this cathedral for the lawyer Marco Mantoa Benavides. Fragments of Mantegna's work, in particular a 'Martyrdom of St Christopher' (which had been removed for safety before the bombing), remain in the Ovetari chapel to the right of the choir. He himself is said to be depicted in the martyrdom.

The Paduans have restored the former Augustinian convent to house their civic museum, with its splendid Giottos, Veroneses, Titians and Tintorettos. Just north of this convent is what was once a Roman amphitheatre and is now a peaceful garden in which rises the Cappella degli Scrovegni. (Taking its cue from the former amphitheatre, this chapel is usually named the Madonna dell'Arena.)

The Cappella degli Scrovegni was built in 1303 by Enrico Scrovegni to atone for the sin of usury committed by his father. Enrico lies in a tomb by Andreolo de' Santi behind the high altar, on which are lovely statues of the Virgin and a couple of angels sculpted by Giovanni Pisano only three years after the church was built. But what makes this chapel magical are its frescos, mostly the work of Giotto, with additions by his pupils. Giotto worked on them from 1303 to 1309, covering the walls with Virtues and Vices, with doctors and elders of the church, prophets and saints, Jesus and his mother, and with a history of human redemption that begins with the expulsion of Joachim from the Temple and ends with the Last Judgement.

Born in Vespignano, close to Florence, around 1267, Giotto is said to have been taken under the wing of Giovanni Cimabue, the most celebrated Florentine painter of that time. The story

115

goes that at the age of ten Giotto was discovered tending sheep by his teacher. His friend Dante, in celebrated lines, declared that Giotto outstripped his master:

> *Credette Cimabue nella pintura*
> *tener lo campo, e ora ha Giotto il grido,*
> *sì che la fama di colui è oscura.*

> (Over the field of painting,
> Cimabue thought to preside, and now Giotto has the cry,
> eclipsing the other's fame.)

Giotto's huge talent encompassed the creation not simply of individual works of art but of series of frescos, whose momentum takes the spectator from one thrill to another. He achieved this in Florence and Assisi, and he supremely mastered it here in Padua.

The rhythm of individual scenes effortlessly crosses the borders of the panels, as for example in the double panel of the Annunciation, where both Mary and the archangel Gabriel are bound together in terms of colour by their plaited golden hair (though the hairdressing is different) and by their red robes (though the reds are different).

Again and again an animal adds a poignant touch to a fresco. Expelled from the Temple, Joachim hugs a little lamb. On a mountain top he sadly approaches a couple of gloomy shepherds and their heedless flock, but a sheepdog offers hope by leaping up to welcome the patriarch. Animals cavort when Joachim makes his sacrifices. They are still around as he dreams. The dumb donkey almost steals the scene when Jesus rides in triumph into Jerusalem.

Giotto's pioneering use of perspective also appears in these frescos, *inter alia* in his architectural details. Another device, by which Giotto refuses to focus on one single figure at the centre of his frescos (as in the Nativity itself), teeters on the brink of failure but ultimately succeeds magnificently. In his

'Adoration of the Magi', for example, the pivot of the fresco is a far post of the stable in which Jesus was born; in the 'Slaughter of the Innocents' Giotto's focus is a dead baby's upturned bottom. Whenever Giotto does revert to the traditional, centrally focused, triangular pattern of a painting, as in his depiction of the flight into Egypt in this chapel, the effect is overpowering.

His faces achieve new heights of expressiveness: contrite Joachim; Mary gazing intently on her new-born son; the mothers' anguish in his depiction of the 'Slaughter of the Innocents'; wondering angels, as Jesus consents to being baptized in the River Jordan; a bibulous guest at the Marriage of Cana; the scowls of Jesus's plotting enemies on the right of the scene where he drives the moneychangers from the Jerusalem Temple.

In Giotto's frescos for the Scrovegni chapel, eyes fix each other, another artistic technique that he superbly developed and deployed. Presented to the priest in the Temple, the infant Jesus looks sapiently at the high priest, who gazes back as if at an ineffable wonder. (Meanwhile Jesus's right arm complements this rhythm by pointing back towards his mother's hands.) When Jesus washes the feet of St Peter, the disciple's eyes protest uncomprehendingly at the loving glance of his Lord. Nowhere in the whole cycle do two persons peer into each other's eyes so closely as when Judas is about to betray his master with a kiss.

Then Giotto's mood changes, as he paints the passion of his Lord. Mocked before Caiaphas, Jesus looks at no one, not even ourselves as we gaze at the fresco. Half-closed, his eyes peer at the ground as he is beaten, whereas Pontius Pilate, washing his hands of the whole affair, looks away. Carrying his cross, the suffering Saviour's eyes are next focused on eternity. And at his crucifixion, while his mother weeps uncontrollably, even the faces of the angels are contorted in despair. As she embraces his dead body, the same angels tear their hair and cry out in pain, their bodies even more contorted than at his crucifixion.

Can angels suffer? Giotto makes them do so. And then,

brilliantly, he sets at the central point of his fresco of the Resurrection not St Mary Magdalene kneeling at the foot of Jesus, not even the risen Jesus himself, but an angel at peace. In between Jesus and Mary Magdalene, leafy little trees symbolize new life, contrasting with two dead stumps (which, of course, may well once have had blossom that has been painted over, though I hope not in the light of my interpretation of this fresco).

The Virtues and Vices painted in this chapel presage the Last Judgement. As ever in such scenes, even for Giotto, the Vices are far more expressive than the Virtues. Rage rips his garments to bare his breast (matching the action of the high priest in the fresco where Jesus is being beaten). Flames of hell are flickering beside Infidelity. They are already burning the legs of Envy, in whose hand is a bag of money and from whose mouth emerges a snake. Likewise in the Last Judgement, the damned are far more vivaciously miserable than the saved are happy. One man hangs from a tree by means of a rope; a woman with sunken dugs hangs by her hair. Beside them their counterparts hang upside-down.

Paduans seem not to have feared this supposedly dread Judgement. One of the city's medieval chroniclers, Rolandino, tells the tale of an amorous woman named Cunizza, a member of the Ezzolini family, who eloped from her first husband in the company of a former lover named Sordello, with whom she lived adulterously. Next she lived at Trevigi with a soldier whose wife also inhabited the same town. Her brother murdered this soldier and married Cunizza off to a nobleman from Braganzo. Soon the same brother had murdered this nobleman, at which Cunizza concluded her final wedding at Verona.

Dante met Sordello in Purgatory. Cunizza, however, he met in Paradise, in the third heaven, namely the planet Venus. She told him she had not cause to regret not being in a higher circle of heaven. Venus, after all, had led her astray on earth, 'And here,' she said, 'I glitter in its light.'

Around Padua villas abound. One of the most impressive for

its sheer size lies eighteen kilometres north-west, in the textile town of Piazzola sul Brenta. Set in a superb park, the central part of Villa Simes (formerly known as Villa Contarini) was built in 1546, traditionally attributed to Palladio. In the 1670s and the nineteenth century the villa gained two lengthy aisles, while a huge hemicycle of outbuildings complete the ensemble. The Carraci family and pupils of Giulio Romano frescoed and painted its many rooms, and you can visit the villa daily except on Mondays.

Drive a further seven kilometres north-west and you reach what was once known as Isola di Carturo. Today the spot is usually called Isola di Mantegna, for the painter Andrea Mantegna was born here in 1431.

Taking the N11 east from Padua towards Venice also reveals more Venetan villas, these set in the valley of the River Brenta. Near Noventa Padovana stand the seventeenth-century Villa Giustiniani, and the Villas Grimani and Giovanelli, the two latter both built in the following century. You can visit Villa Giovanelli, if you telephone in advance (049-625066), and the effort is well worth while. Antonio Gaspari began the villa and Giorgio Massari enlarged it in 1738, in honour of a visit by Maria Amalia, the daughter of King Frederick Augustus of Poland. The salon on the first floor was frescoed in the mid-eighteenth century by Giovanni Angeli, and the rest retains its frescos of 1738. Massari also supervised the planting of a new garden in 1738, with its maze and little temple.

Just outside Strà the Brenta enters the province of Venezia. Here the huge Villa Pisani is mirrored in the river. This is the largest of all the Venetan villas and so vast and sumptuous that it is often known as Villa Royale. You can visit it daily except on Mondays. Built by F. M. Preti around two courtyards (some decorated, some not) on behalf of the Pisani, whose family supplied doges for Venice, the building was completed when Alviso Pisano was elected doge in 1735. On its front façade four caryatids hold up the balcony, while Corinthian pilasters are carried by terrific atlantes to a cornice of putti and swags of fruit underneath an escutcheoned pediment.

Villa Pisani was decorated in the eighteenth century by artists of the calibre of Giambattista Tiepolo, whose masterpiece here is a brilliantly organized apotheosis of the Pisani family, painted for the ballroom in 1762. As ever, his cherubs are overweight. Here too are mementoes of Napolean Bonaparte and Mussolini, a chapel, and a room with ceramics depicting the doges of Venice. *Trompe-l'oeil* classical doorways and grisaille panels enhance a villa which covers 5,000 square metres and which, on the main floor, encompasses twenty-two rooms.

Yet there is a sense of desolation inside, and I prefer its magnificent park, though on my visits its maze, celebrated in Gabriele d'Annunzio's novel *The Fire*, has always borne the dread notice *Chiuso per impractabilita da Pioggia* (closed on account of rain). Radiating alleyways all end at some delicious feature. Pavilions boast eighteenth-century statuary. Ornamental gateways include two approached by wisteria-clad pergolas. A chestnut avenue leads from another gateway to the garden. On a moated mound rises a gazebo.

'If one may build upon a river, it will be both convenient and beautiful,' declared Palladio himself. His reason was, as ever, first of all a practical one: 'because at all times, and with little expense, the products may be convey'd to the city in boats, and will serve for the uses of the house and cattle'. In addition, he added, rivers serve to afford a beautiful prospect, to cool the air in summer and enable the estate, pleasure and kitchen gardens ('the sole and chief recreation of a villa') to be watered 'with great utility and ornament'.

From Vitruvius he handed on tips for determining whether or not the waters were good: 'That water is deemed perfect which makes good bread, and in which greens are quickly boiled; and which, being boiled, does not leave any fur or sediment at the bottom of the vessel.' Sand and gravel at the bottom of a river, rather than mud, were another indication of decent water, Palladio added. So was an absence of moss and rushes, as well as lively, robust and fat animals drinking from the rivers. Such enquiries were all the more vital since, he observed, 'Some bad waters generate the spleen, others glandulous swellings in the neck, others the stone, and many other diseases.'

The Brenta was the most convenient river for conveying the Venetian nobility and their visitors from Venice to the country-side. Joseph Addison took only one day to travel from Padua to Venice. Half a century earlier John Evelyn recorded sailing in a horse-drawn barge for twenty miles along the same river, 'The country on both sides deliciously adorn'd with country villas and gentlemen's requirements, gardens planted with oranges, figs and other fruit belonging to the Venetians'. Today you can sail from Padua to Venice on *Il Burchiello*, a modern version of the seventeenth- and eighteenth-century boats, while a multilingual guide points to the superb villas on either side of the river.

The journey from Strà towards Venice proffers one after another of these exquisite buildings. As well as Villa Pisani, Strà boasts the seventeenth-century Villa Zanetti, frescoed by A. Urbani; the seventeenth-century Palazzo Cappello; and, from the same era, Villa Foscarini with its classical relief, frescoed by P. Liberi and D. Bruni.

A few metres from Villa Pisani stands Villa Soranza, a sixteenth-century, three-storey building by G. B. Cipriani. On the other side of the river stretches the long, grey eighteenth-century Villa Reconnati-Zucconi, looking like a yellow-and-white china dolls' house. Further along the placid river stands on the right the eighteenth-century Villa Contarini. And so they go on, signposted to left and right (often with erroneous information about opening times and inconsistent names) towards Venice.

The Brenta canal veers south-east. Follow the river to discover that, at Mira, the local library is housed in a villa built in 1588. Between 1817 and 1819 Byron stayed at Mira in the Foscarini palace, where he composed the fourth quarto of his

Childe Harold. Here too he first met Margherita Cogni, whom he dubbed 'La bella Fornarina'.

Outside Mira stands Villa Widman, built in 1719 and once the home of Cardinal Rezzonico (who became Pope Clement XIII) and the playwright Carlo Goldoni. You can visit this villa daily except on Mondays. The pretty cube of a building turns its back on the main road to overlook its garden, little fountain and statues. The entrance hall, though small, has most lively frescos, as well as Murano chandeliers and green silk tapestry, while other rooms have delicately painted ceilings and cornices. The stables still house carriages and tack. Further on in the garden you can enjoy a lake, a gazebo, seats, handsome trees and quiet walks.

Across the road and the water rise the long, low lines of the seventeenth-century Barchese Valmanara. And just beyond Oriago (which is blessed by the Villa Gradenigo), turn right along the road to Fusina to find the lovely Villa Foscari, which Palladio built in 1571 for Niccolò and Luigi Foscari. An inscription over the door records that in 1574 the Foscari entertained here Henry III, King of France and Poland. Such frescos as survive are by G. B. Franco and G. B. Zelotti. Palladio paid tribute to the former thus: 'Messer Battista Franco, a very great designer of our times, had begun to paint one of the great rooms; but being overtaken by death, has left the work imperfect.' Palladio's designs raised the main building eleven feet off the ground, placing below it the kitchens and servants' quarters.

Villa Foscari is nicknamed 'La Malcontenta' after a woman who is said to have been confined here after being found faithless to her husband. Warming to this legend, Georgina Masson observed, 'In a curious fashion the name so expresses the *genius loci* of the villa, which is often wreathed with mists even on a bright summer morning, that its adoption is not surprising.' Visitors are welcome from April to October in the mornings (although not on Sundays and Mondays).

A third entrancing excursion from Padua is to explore the Euganean hills, with their numerous spas, their rich vineyards, their orchards and their fields of tobacco and cereals. Leave the city by Via dei Colli and drive south-west towards Teolo. After ten kilometres there appears on the right Montecchia di Selvazzano, where Villa Emo Capodilista stands on a rise in another glorious park made more delightful by the surrounding vineyards. Dario Varotari designed it in two storeys, faced with open loggias, in the late sixteenth century, and the mannerist Il'Aliense painted its galleries and walls in the 1770s on the themes of vines, architecture and villas. A minimum of twenty-five persons is required for a visit (telephone 049-650512).

Beside the villa is a golf course laid out by Tom Macaulay, chairman of the British Association of Golf Architects. Opposite the gate is the *fattoria* where sometimes (I think on Wednesdays and Saturdays, but one is never sure in this part of the Veneto) you can buy the local Montecchia DOC wines.

Scarcely three kilometres further on you reach San Biagio, just south of which an avenue of trees leads to the superb abbey of Praglia. Already you are among steep, forest-covered hills that resemble overgrown hedgehogs. Though founded around 1080 by Benedictines, the abbey was almost entirely rebuilt in the fifteenth and sixteenth centuries. Despite the fact that its name derives from the Latin for meadowland (*pratalea*), the abbey of Praglia is perfectly sheltered by the surrounding hills. The monks run guided tours, through the sixteenth-century botanical cloister, with its palms and roses; the upper cloister, with its painted Renaissance arcades and well; stuccoed rooms; the abbot's quarters (on longer tours), with paintings by Pozzoserrato; the double cloister of 1469 (likewise on longer tours); the sixteenth-century chapter house; the *chiostro rustico*, whose rooms were designed for the hospitality that monks are supposed always to offer; and, above all, the refectory.

This last is a marvel. After washing in the seventeenth-century lavabo ouside, monks would enter through Tullio Lombardo's doorway into a long room created in 1726, comprising on three sides walnut veneer, over which are intricately carved crests. Each one embodies elaborate symbolism. In one Samson pulls down the temple of the Philistines (a symbol of fortitude). In another justice is represented by the judgement of Solomon. Pears punctured by wasps reminded the monks that little faults can result in ruin, or *A Parvo exitum*, as the inscription reads. Another inscription, *Humilior quo onustior*, accompanies a laden fruit tree, whose boughs bend the more they carry – just as, the greater virtue a monk has, the deeper is his humility.

On one crest a fish gasps miserably, a symbol of those who perish when they leave the presence of God. A horny-shelled chestnut reminds the monks of the aim of discipline: under the husk is sweetness. Maybe we all can learn from the crest of roses carved with thorns and from its motto *Non sine altera*: no joy without pain. A good number of these crests pursue this theme: an orange is squeezed, for without it there is no juice; a dolphin exults in a storm; other dolphins fearfully return to their mother, just as stormy weather makes us return to God; a harp illustrates the motto *Sonus ex ictibus*, meaning that good results can come from blows.

Although, being devoutly inclined, I agree with all this, I also think that but for the exquisiteness of the carvings one could have too much along these lines. More to my taste is the slumbering lion whose motto declares that, even asleep, he meditates on God (*Nec in somno quies*), and I commend the motto of a bear licking its cub, *Lambendo reformat*: you enrich more with gentleness than severity. A carving of an overloaded camel, with the motto *Ne supra vires* (do not take on more than you can bear) reinforces my point.

Two early sixteenth-century works of art conclude those in this refectory: Tullio Lombardo's marble pulpit and Bartolomeo Montagna's sombre fresco of the crucifixion. The monastery also has two libraries, in lovely rooms, and as you walk around, do not forget to look out of the windows at its garden of orange trees, roses and vines.

We owe the design of the white-façaded monastery church,

which rises from a piazza at the top of a monumental flight of steps, also to Tullio Lombardo, who began the building in 1497. It was finished in 1548, sixteen years after his death. Inside are paintings by such contemporary Venetians as Zelotti and L. Longhi.

On the way to Teolo a road running to the left of Treponti leads to the sterner but extremely fine Villa dei Vescovi at Luvigliano. Giovanni Maria Falconetto built it in the sixteenth century for Cardinal Pisani, Bishop of Padua. It looks like an icing-cake bungalow with a double staircase and a stone balustrade. To visit the villa you must telephone in advance (049-5211118), otherwise remaining content to buy the local products, including a great variety of local wines, on sale outside. In Treponti itself look out for the turning on the right that leads to Frassanelle, where woods shelter the nineteenth-century Villa Papafava.

Two of the region's most celebrated writers – though men separated in time by thirteen centuries – spent some of their lives in this part of the Veneto. In 59 BC the quiet village of Teolo was the birthplace of Livy. On the way there the road winds steeply through forests and up the now dramatic hills. Then it descends, snaking through vineyards.

Turn left just beyond Zovon towards Este, driving until a sign points you left into the Euganean Hills Natural Park, and arrive shortly at Valnogaredo. Stone statues top the walls guarding Villa Contarini. In the eighteenth century Guarana frescoed its interior, as well as the parish church opposite. A road winds up the hill to the left of the village to reach the medieval castle built by the Carraresi family.

You shall shortly reach one of the finest gardens in this part of Italy. Continue towards a main road and turn left towards Galzignano Terme. Here a signpost on the right directs you to Valsanzibio. In 1669 Antonio Barbarigo, procurator of the republic of Venice, built the villa here that bears his name. Waterfalls and fountains, statues and tree-lined alleyways enliven the huge garden.

'I have not seen any gardens in Italy worth taking notice of,' wrote John Evelyn after his visit to the Veneto in the mid-seventeenth century. His remark is extraordinary. For over 150 years Italian Renaissance gardens had been among the most creative in Europe. The science of gardening was part of the new learning and, as we have already seen, Padua's botanical garden was exquisite as well as useful. The loggias of villas generally led out to them, their windows opening out on to the vistas that Titian so loved to include in his paintings. Orange trees and potted palms softened the harsh contours.

New-found engineering skills enabled gardeners to control the flow of water, skills that entranced Leonardo da Vinci. A hillside park thus became a prized asset to any villa. Roman statues would surround pools. The contents of pools and rivers gave inspiration to garden sculptors. The brilliant Renaissance architect Leon Battista Alberti (whom Palladio so admired and who designed the Boboli gardens in Florence) even proposed smearing sculpted shells with wax to suggest age. Grottoes reflected the wildness of the countryside – even its dangers – while sculpted figures among them suggested human control.

Villa Barbarigo has just such a garden, its ambience all the more breathtaking because of the wooded Euganean hills that surround it on three sides. From the beginning of March until the end of November you can visit this garden, though not the villa, from 09.30 to 12.00 and from 14.00 to 18.00 (except on Sundays and Monday mornings). A classic feature of Renaissance gardens is its central dividing axis, created out of falling water. The waters run down to pools with a fanciful stone gateway topped with a statue of Diana the huntress. Huge box hedges frame the way up to the villa, beyond which a row of cypresses rises to the top of the hill. Set amid ancient trees and dense foliage, the garden paths lead to a huge box maze (with a gazebo in the middle, where the lost could work out how to escape). Secret entrances beckon you into the shady hideaway, with stone seats and statues. A circular moated arbour, with ducks and swans, surrounds an aviary.

126

Twisting south-east from here, make your way to the hilltown of Arquà Petrarca. Here Petrarch, the second of the region's famous writers, lived and died. His red marble sarcophagus, set up in front of the parish church of Santa Maria in 1380, six years after his death, is still here. The church has Romanesque frescos and a coffered roof. And in the upper part of the village is the house where Petrarch lived from 1370 to his death. He built it on land given to him by his friend Francesco il Vecchio da Carrara. It is now his memorial, and among those who pilgrimaged here and signed the visitors' book were Byron, Shelley and Mozart. Petrarch worshipped not in Santa Maria but in the oratory of Santi Trinità, whose beautiful courtyard opens up near his home.

The way back to Padua is signposted in Arquà Petrarca. Three noted Venetan spas now beckon. Sitting on either side of a canal dug by the Paduans in 1201 (to bring building materials from the Euganean hills), the medieval town of Battáglia Terme has been reputed for its waters since the Middle Ages. Among its treasures is Villa Selvatico Emo Capodilista, built in the early years of the seventeenth century, with a scenic staircase of 1646 in a park laid out afresh in 1818 by G. Japelli. (Telephone 049-8721650 for a visit.) Drive due east across the motorway to reach, after three and a half kilometres, Carrara Santo Stéfano, whose church dates from the tenth century and has a thirteenth-century belfry. Inside is the fourteenth-century marble tomb of Marsilio da Carrara.

Montegrotto Terme lies five kilometres north of Battáglia Terme. On the way the road passes, at Cataio, the powerful Castello degli Obizzi, which the Venetian admiral Pio Enea II degli Obizzi had built in 1570. Once its external walls were covered with delicate frescos, but these are sadly dilapidated and almost obliterated. Inside remain fine frescos painted by G. B. Zelotti in 1571. A quaint feature of the garden is its elephant fountain.

Montegrotto Terme draws on the same thermal springs as Battáglia Terme. The Romans knew them, alleging that the God Aponus here suffused them with his healing powers. Today guests at these spas are covered with a clay known as *fango*, described in some literature I picked up from the spa authorities as 'a brownish-grey, plastic, soapy mush'. No doubt it improves the health of the guests, as certainly do the splendid sporting facilities on offer and the superb countryside.

A road to the west leads up to the glorious panorama of Padua and Venice itself, which is revealed from the 416-metre-high Monte Rua. Here in 1339 a hermitage was built, and rebuilt in 1537. Its inhabitants allow only male visitors.

The third celebrated Euganean spa, Abano Terme, lies hardly four kilometres north of Montegrotto Terme and ten kilometres south of Padua, its resident population swollen enormously by those seeking the solace of its curative mud baths. Before returning to the city, make a brief excursion west to Monteortone, whose fifteenth-century sanctuary has frescos by Jacopo da Montagnana.

Treviso and the joyful province

At the confluence of the Rivers Sile and Botteniga (which calls itself the Cagnan inside the city walls), Treviso lies in the fertile Venetian plain, scarcely half an hour's drive from Venice. Holidaying here, the eighteenth-century Venetian dramatist Carlo Goldoni declared that 'se spassiza, se zoga, se ciacola e qualche volta se incantona' ('one walks, one plays, one converses and sometimes goes off with an enchanting woman'), and I confirm that this is the best way of enjoying this most delightful city. The drive from Venice is pleasant enough, but far more enjoyable is the sail from the lagoon up the River Sile. Like Venice, Treviso is channelled and lapped by water, here the streams that flow from the Botteniga into the Sile. Unlike Venice, Treviso is also walled, its bastions dating from the fifteenth and sixteenth centuries, the embankment of its moat filled with vegetation and greenery.

The Venetians paid for these walls, approximately five kilometres of them, and the embankment too, commissioning the Veronese engineer Fra Giovanni Giocondo to build them in the early sixteenth century. Their aim was to make Treviso a bulwark against their enemies, who had formed the League of Cambrai.

This belligerent stance has left an enviably calm circuit of ramparts with gun embrasures, crumbling brick walls moulded with white Istrian marble, hydraulic engineering (designed to protect Treviso from attack by flooding the surrounding countryside) and three defensive gates, which nevertheless contrived at the same time to be works of art. They overlook iridescent green waters, occasionally flanked by rows of horse chestnuts, and from time to time the walls are decorated with crests and Istrian stone lions.

Without impertinence to the other beauties of the city, I find the gates of Treviso among its most beguiling monuments. Porta San Tomaso, covered in Istrian stone, was built by Guglielmo Bergamasco in 1518. Its name derives from Archbishop Thomas à Becket of Canterbury, since in this quarter of Treviso used to stand a church dedicated in his honour. The Venetian governor at that time, Paolo Nani, wanted the gate named after his own patron saint and he got part of his wish, for the statue on top of its lead-clad cupola does depict St Paul, identified by his traditional sword (representing the one that decapitated him).

Bergamasco built a triumphal classical arch, its six Corinthian columns rising on plinths and flanking trophies, escutcheons, ribbons and cuirasses. The lion of St Mark, his paw resting on a copy of Mark's Gospel, growls above the arch. On either side of the lion are slits that once accommodated the chains of the drawbridge. 'Porta San Tomaso' is carved in the Venetian dialect on the arch. The inscription on the inside reads 'Dominus custodiat introitum et exitum tuum' ('The Lord preserve thy going out and thy coming in'), a quotation from Psalm 121, verse 8. Flanking the statue of the Madonna and child on the southern wall are St Liberale and the Blessed Enrico, both patrons of Treviso.

Porta dei Santi Quaranti guards the west side of the city. Alessandro Vendramin built it in 1517, and decided that its inscription should praise himself. This is a less flamboyant gateway than Porta San Tomaso, although once again the winged lion of St Mark stands above its arch, again flanked with slits for the drawbridge chains. The façade, clad in Istrian marble, has four massive pilasters. Porta Altina is the third surviving gate, protecting the southern flank of the town and close to a square bastion. This stone archway is formidable, carrying a tower, though less ornate than the other two.

Like many a town in this region, Treviso was given city status by the Romans, in this case in 89 BC, and once again you can see the Roman street pattern surviving in the present layout – the former *Cardus Maximus* running along today's Calmaggiore, Via Indipendenza and Via Santa Margerita, the *Decumanus* along Via Martiri della Libertà. Treviso escaped the depradations of Attila the Hun and managed to prosper under Goth and Lombard rule. The thirteenth and fourteenth centuries were less secure, with tyrants and then the Guelphs dominating the city. The Venetians, the Austrians and the Carraresi family all felt it better that Treviso should be subject to their rule, rather than live as a free commune.

Yet, in spite of these problems, Treviso attracted artists of the calibre of Lorenzo Lotto, Tommaso da Modena and Pietro and Tullio Lombardo. Its native-born master was Girolamo da Treviso the Elder. Venetian Gothic characterizes its dwellings, some of which are tapestried with external frescos.

Its citizens have continued to delight in the abundance of water, so that in the triangular Piazza Sant'Andrea for instance, with its eighteenth-century church and frescoed houses, gushes a modern fountain and a little stepped waterfall. In mid-Lent crowds of Trevisans enjoy a watery festival known in their dialect as the trial of the old lady (the *Processo alla Vecia*). This bizarre event involves a dummy whose ugly features represent everything bad that has affected the citizens over the past year. Once tried, the old woman is sentenced to death and hung over the water from the Ponte Santa Margherita. Then intrepid Trevisans leap into the river and set her on fire with torches.

The heart of the city is the delightfully irregular Piazza dei Signori. In the midst of its many vicissitudes, Treviso was a self-governing commune from the twelfth century until, in 1389, its citizens threw in their lot with the republic of Venice, and three sides of this piazza are lined with pink-brick buildings from that era. On the east side rises the massive Romanesque Palazzo dei Trecento, battlemented and dating from 1217. Mullioned windows lighten its severity. Its arcaded loggia was added in 1552. This palace stands on the site of Treviso's Roman forum, and rightly so, because here in the huge upper hall (which measures forty-seven by twenty metres) would deliberate some 300 councillors from the city and province. Romanesque hunting and love scenes still decorate its walls, as does a frieze dating from 1500 depicting the coats of arms of the Venetian governors of the city. The roof has powerful double-trusses, supported by carved joists. In summer its arcades shade tables and chairs where the citizens munch *porchetta* (warm pork) sandwiches bought at neighbouring cafés and washed down with beer.

Beside the Palazzo dei Trecento stands the Palazzo del Podestà of 1491, its tower (the Torre del Commune) rising askew. On the opposite side of the piazza stands the former Palazzo Pretorio, while the eastern side of Palazzo dei Trecento shades the Piazza Indipendenza, which centres on a statue of independence (created by Luigi Borro in 1871) known irreverently to the Trevisans as Fat Theresa. This side of the *palazzo*, like the others, is battlemented and arcaded, the second floor reached by an open-air staircase.

Piazza dei Signori thus sets the scene for the whole city, with its narrow, arcaded streets flanked by ancient homes and paved with square cobblestones known as sets. From the piazza, Via Barbiere curves slenderly away. To another side in Piazza del Monte di Pietà you can visit the Monte di Pietà with its late sixteenth-century Rettori chapel. Around 1580 the Flemish-born artist dubbed Ludovico Pozzoserrato by the Trevisans painted the scenes depicting six acts of charity, which hang in richly gilded frames on its walls. Though these are all biblical stories, Pozzoserrato set some of them in Venetan villas. The chapel has a beamed ceiling with painted tracery, while the wall-covering, gilded and silvered in the Arabic-Spanish style, is of Cordovan leather. Girolamo da Treviso the Elder painted the chapel's 'Falling asleep of the Blessed Virgin' in 1748.

Close by is the Loggia dei Cavalieri, commissioned in the late thirteenth century by governor Andrea da Perugia as a meeting place for the Trevisan nobility. Under its frescoed court – five-arched on three sides and rising from slender stone columns – the nobility would converse, play chess and plot. These days they have been supplanted by booksellers, flower stalls, toy merchants and antique dealers.

In autumn the Piazza del Monte di Pietà is filled with stalls selling mushrooms, the most prized being the *ciodeto (Armillariella mellea)* and the *brisoti (Boletus edulis)*, which grow on the wooded Montello, a hill to the north of the city. Beside its Loggia dei Cavalieri, through an archway leading into Piazza San Vito, you reach the churches of Santa Lucia and San Vito. The former was built in 1389 to mark Treviso's subjection to Venice (which was formally ratified on the Feast of St Lucy), and was frescoed in the fourteenth century by Tommaso da Modena, the most important painter to work in this city. Three-aisled, with Gothic vaulting, the first chapel on the right abuts on to the Romanesque chancel of San Vito. The most celebrated painting in this church is Tommaso da Modena's 'Madonna del Pavegio', in which baby Jesus, sitting on her knee, is trying to catch a butterfly.

Built in the twelfth century and partially rebuilt in 1561, San Vito boasts an arcaded portico. Here too are frescos, these ones dating from the twelfth and thirteenth centuries and depicting the lives of saints, as well as a late fourteenth-century crucifixion, a Madonna by Tommaso da Modena, and a pretty painting by M. Vercellio. A stone tabernacle, dating from the fourteenth century, is carved with a complex Gothic bas-relief of 1363, which depicts the heads of saints and portraits of the donors. The oldest frescos of all are those in the little eleventh- and twelfth-century chancel chapel.

The city's finest street, Calmaggiore, with its arcades and

fifteenth- and sixteenth-century houses, runs from the other side of Piazza dei Signori as far as the cathedral, in whose piazza grow magnolias. The varied columns of its arcades are worth stroking, while the façades of the shops have fragmentary Gothic and Renaissance frescos. Running off from this street, Via Bianchetta boasts a thirteenth-century medieval house, and in Via Cornarotta a thirteenth-century Romanesque tower rises above sixteenth- and seventeenth-century houses.

Treviso's cathedral was founded in the twelfth century, but was subsequently much altered. Its apse was rebuilt in the fifteenth and sixteenth centuries, and most of the rest in the eighteenth. The neo-classical façade with its huge, and slightly out-of-place, six-columned portico dates from 1838. Yet, with its seven lead-covered cupolas and its massive brick campanile (which was begun in the eleventh century and finished in the next), this is no miserable building. Two Romanesque lions flank the cathedral steps, carved from red Verona marble. One of them, with an exceedingly curly tail, is killing a serpent. These lions formerly supported the portico of Treviso's first cathedral.

Inside, the three aisles with their powerful pillars were created by Giordano Riccati in 1760 and house many treats, including an 'Adoration of the Magi' by Paris Bordone on the second altar in the right aisle. The finest works of art are in the Cappella dell'Annunziata, including on its altar an 'Annunciation' of 1523 by Titian himself.

Here Titian was not content to paint a conventional Annunciation. The angel swoops in from the right, on powerful wings, his white robe matched by the Virgin's lily, which he carries in his left hand. Mary turns away from him, still unwilling to bear the son of God, though she turns her head obediently towards the heavenly messenger. The curious little figure who crouches half-hidden behind a Corinthian basilica seems quite out of place in this painting but happens to be Canon Malschiostro, who commissioned it. In this same chapel is a 'Virgin and Saints' done in 1487 by Girolamo da Treviso. The Virgin holds a flower, which her *bambino* reaches out for. Two cherubs languidly play instruments. On the left a near-naked St Sebastian is about to swoon from the pain of the arrows that pierce his body. On the right St James the Great, staff in hand, cockleshell on his hat, script hanging by his side, is about to set off for Santiago de Compostela. In this lovely painting St James is the only saint customarily portrayed wearing boots, since he is a pilgrim.

In a single day in 1520 Pordenone frescoed for this chapel a brilliant 'Adoration of the Magi' and an equally splendid 'Visitation', which display in their style his admiration for Michelangelo. Fretted stone screens, stalls and inlay work add more richness, along with an 'Adoration of the Shepherds', painted by Paris Bordone in 1557.

Renaissance architecture first appears in this cathedral in the Cappella Maggiore of 1488, the work of Pietro Lombardo. Another splendid chapel houses the Holy Sacrament. Created by Pietro Lombardo in 1513, it contains sculptures by him and also by Tullio Lombardo. Pietro and his sons Tullio and Antonio made the impressive Renaissance tomb of Bishop Zanetto, who died in 1486. Pietro Lombardo also designed the high altar of the cathedral.

A fine sculpture from another era is the baroque monument to Pope Alexander VIII, which Giovanni Bonazza created in 1693. Alexander, who had died two years previously, was a tough Pope when it came to repudiating the pretensions of Louis XIV of France to rule the French church. A Venetian by birth, he annoyed the papal states by giving money, troops and galleys to La Serenissima in support of her war against the Turks, and pleased them by reducing taxes and importing cheap food. Aged seventy-nine when elected Pope, he used to say he had to work fast, since he had already reached the twenty-third hour. One result of this haste was the remarkable number of rich benefices and offices that he gave to his relatives. He liked writers (a virtue for which no one can be praised enough). His monument is as ostentatious as was his life.

The apse of Treviso's cathedral was frescoed by Pier Maria Pennacchi in 1511. But all these delights (save for Titian's 'Annunciation') pale beside the beauty of the columned crypt, built in the eleventh and twelfth centuries, some of its capitals cannibalized from an earlier eighth-century building. The Romanesque mosaic pavement depicts horrid-looking beasts. One of Treviso's patron saints, Liberale, lies here in a sarcophagus of 1403.

Walk past the cathedral to find another Romanesque marvel, the red-brick baptistry. Its door retains the original thirteenth-century woodwork. The friezes on either side are Roman, sculpted in the third or fourth century. Inside are frescos painted from the twelfth to the fourteenth centuries. The finest is a thirteenth-century, Byzantine-style portrait of the Madonna and child, between the archangel Gabriel and St Prosdocimus. As for the campanile, it dates basically from the thirteenth century and seems in a very grumpy mood.

Piazza del Duomo also contains the Vescovado, the episcopal palace, which has sixteenth-century frescos by Benedetto Caliari illustrating the parables of Jesus. If you walk under its spacious arch you find the remains of a fourth-century Roman mosaic, with lively birds perching on vines which cupids are about to consume. The Palazzo del Tribunale in the same piazza was erected here in the nineteenth century.

Via Canova, enhanced by more frescoed façades (including that of the Venetian Gothic Casa da Noal, with its sixteenth-century courtyard, Gothic well and open staircase), runs from here to one of Treviso's two excellent museums. The Museo della Casa Trevignia is the city's gallery of decorative and applied arts. A fifteenth-century Gothic building, it displays ceramics, sculptures, furniture and musical instruments from the Middle Ages to the eighteenth century. No. 18 nearby is a lovely Renaissance house decorated with the frescos that add a special nuance to Treviso. And a little further on (at no. 22 Borgo Cavour) is the civic museum. Its prize artist is Tommaso da Modena, his finest work here a cycle depicting the life of St Ursula; but here too are works by Titian, Bassano, Cima da Conegliano and Tiepolo. But perhaps Trevisans prefer, above all, their local sculptor Arturo Martini's portrait of Lillian Gish. The baroque church opposite the museum is dedicated to Saint Agnes, its seventeenth-century baroque façade by Andrea Pagnossin. Inside are some not too ostentatious baroque altars.

It you walk back from here to Via Canova you will find, to your horror, that the seventeenth-century All Saints' convent has been deconsecrated and given over to tax offices, thus (some might say) converting the house of God into a den of thieves. At Ponte di San Chiliano turn into Via Roggia, which runs alongside a canal and is lined with colonnaded houses, some of them frescoed. The street reaches Piazza Trenti, whence shady arches and little bridges lead to Vicolo del Gallo and one of the sweetest parts of Treviso, the Buranelli. Its name derives from fishermen who came here from the island of Burano. Here an arched passageway is reflected in the water of the gentle Cagnan di Mezzo.

The way west to the church of San Francesco takes in the heady succession of Piazza Rinaldi, with its Renaissance houses, the Cagnan Grande (where the water turns the wheels of an ancient mill) and the Campagna bridge.

Franciscans reached Treviso in 1216, and they began building their church in 1231, shortly after the canonization of St Francis himself. It was finished in 1270, its austere Romanesque interior enlivened by ogival arches. From the start the Franciscans decorated their church with frescos, the finest being those of Tommaso dei Barsini – who came here from Modena in 1352 and is in consequence known as Tommaso da Modena – in the first and second chapels on the left of the choir. Among the tombs in this church, two are those of children of Italy's greatest writers. Francesca, daughter of Petrarch, who died in childbirth in 1384, lies at the foot of the fourth pillar on the right; Pietro, Dante's son, who died suddenly at Treviso in 1364, lies in the left transept.

Napoleon Bonaparte closed down the monastery in 1806 and, apart from the church, the buildings were destroyed. Napoleon

137

nearly ruined the church as well, transforming it into stables and a quartermaster's stores. It was restored and handed back to the Minor Friars only in 1928, after many masterpieces had disappeared. The tomb of Dante's son, made by the Venetian sculptor Filiberto de Sanctis, was painstakingly restored from fragments in 1935. Other survivors of the Napoleonic vandalism are a huge, late thirteenth-century St Christopher, on the left wall of the nave, as well as a Madonna and seven saints, painted by Tommaso da Modena in the first chapel on the left.

Via San Parisio, with its overhanging houses, runs south from San Francesco to the Pescheria. Here, on an island in the Cagnan Grande, is the venue of a daily fishmarket, shaded by chestnut trees. Stalls selling fruit and vegetables are covered by huge umbrellas in the Via Pescheria. And close by in Via Palestro their owners and shoppers refresh themselves in the lively bars. Façades with Gothic and Renaissance frescos line the street, while through three arches lies the Piazzetta San Parisio.

To the east is the oval rococo church of San Agostino, designed by Francesco Vecelli in the mid-eighteenth century. Inside, rococo stucco curls, and the ceiling depicts the 'Glory of San Girolamo', painted by Antonio Marinetti. The finest altarpiece is Pozzoserrato's 'Madonna of the Celeghri'. Balconied houses line the arcaded Via San Agostino, one of them frescoed with a judgement of Paris. At the end of this street, Piazza Matteoti plays host to a market on Tuesdays and Saturdays. This piazza is familiarly known as Piazza del Grano, on account of the wheat, barley and maize that used to be sold here. Close by rises the church of Santa Caterina.

Santa Caterina, whose façade has a slender mullioned window, once served a monastery that was begun here in 1346. Napoleon again wreaked havoc here, and the monastery and church served as a barracks and military stores under his regime, under the Austrians, and then under the Italians themselves until 1944. Only then did Treviso become aware of the riches inside the church, in particular its superb series of Gothic frescos painted between 1350 and 1400. They include a cycle depicting the legend of St Ursula by Tommaso da Modena, painted between 1353 and 1366. Another fresco, on the right-hand wall, shows St Catherine holding a model of the city.

I have wandered a long time beside the canals of Treviso, lingering in the city's restaurants and sipping its wine (the local treat being a harmonious white known as Ombra). Trevisans often begin their fairly substantial meals with a *risotto*, which varies from season to season, laced with peas or asparagus, liver or chicken, hops or spinach. Other favourite starters are a bean soup, which you discover is warming a pork sausage (a dish known here as *sopa de fagioli*), which I like very much; tripe in a broth flavoured with rosemary *(sopa di trippa)*, which I abominate; and the excellent *sopa coada*, a meat broth in which swim layers of bread, slices of pigeon meat and grated parmesan.

Eel and trout from the rivers of Treviso grace the tables of this city's restaurants. *Bollito* (boiled meat) is another customary main course. Guinea fowl in spicy *pevarada* sauce or goose with celery may appear on menus. And, more cherished than all the rest, the Trevisan's classic vegetable is red-leaved chicory, *radicchio rosso di Treviso*, cramming baskets everywhere in the city when it is gathered in December. The Piazza dei Signori is the venue of an annual chicory festival, which takes place on the last Tuesday before Christmas. *Radicchio rosso* is usually served raw, dressed in oil and vinegar, sprinkled with salt and pepper, though Giovanni Marchiori's excellent pamphlet *Il Radicchio Rosso di Treviso*, as well as giving hints on its cultivation and detailing the parasites that prey on this delicacy, devotes no fewer than seven pages to traditional chicory recipes. Oddly enough, the Trevisans eschew the *radicchio rosso* when eating the spiced *musetto* sausage, preferring horseradish instead.

Some specialities appear only at religious festivals. Pancakes and little bows of pasta *(fritole* and *crostoli)* are eaten at the beginning of Lent; buns known as *focaccia* are munched at Easter; summer festivals are celebrated with the coloured *bussolai*, a kind of doughnut; little sweets made from crushed pine kernels, sugar, flour, eggs and almonds (*fave*, as they are called) support the citizens on All Souls' Day; while at Christmas they eat nougat.

As well as those we have seen, there are other churches worth exploring here, in particular the little medieval San Gregorio, the thirteenth-century, much rebuilt Santa Margherita, and Santa Maria Maggiore. The last of the three, its gable end curving seductively, has a fifteenth-century nave and a chancel rebuilt in the 1520s by Zaccaria da Lugano. Its miracle-working statue of the Madonna, carved in the fourteenth century, is housed in a marble, gem-encrusted shrine of 1492. The church houses another curiosity too: the fetters from which the Venetian captain Girolamo Emiliano was miraculously released when the imperial forces had imprisoned him. And in the semicircular baptistry are frescos of 1540 by Ludovico Fiumicelli, their theme culminating in Jesus's resurrection.

Another noble church is Giordano Riccati's San Teonosto, whose Corinthian pillars support a triangular pediment. One might omit these churches from a short visit to Treviso, but no one should miss San Niccolò, which is the city's most important Gothic church. Dating from the thirteenth and fourteenth centuries, San Niccolò was built by the Dominicans, and it shares the same awesome proportions that we have seen in their church at Verona.

Dominican monks came to Treviso in 1221 and at first needed only a modest church. Their expectations were transformed, however, when one of their number became Pope Benedict XI in 1303. Benedict, born Niccolò Boccasino to a humble Treviso family of notaries in 1240, became a Dominican as a teenager. A scholar and an acute biblical commentator, by 1286 he was the Dominican Provincial for Lombardy and ten years later a cardinal. The Oxford historian and theologian J. N. D. Kelly describes Benedict as weak, peace-loving and scholarly (though I assume only the first adjective is meant to be pejorative). Dr Kelly adds that Benedict felt at ease only with Dominicans. In his short reign as supreme pontiff (he died of dysentery, or maybe from poison, in 1304) Benedict created only three cardinals, all of them Dominicans. But during his papacy, with two donations amounting to 70,000 gold florins, he persuaded his fellow-monks to begin building the present Gothic masterpiece in his home town.

Its interior is some eighty-five metres long and some thirty metres high. Twelve columns support the ceiling and also, as the Dominicans insisted, represent the twelve apostles supporting their order. Narrow windows soar up to a symbolic heaven. Tommaso da Modena and his pupils decorated its pillars with frescos. Girolamo da Treviso and his pupils painted a 'Doubting Thomas' for the chapel to the right of the choir, which was frescoed in the fourteenth century. Renaissance and baroque altars (the finest devoted to St Roch and the Madonna of the Rosary) fail to intrude on the essential austerity of the building; nor does the beautifully carved Renaissance tomb of Agostino Anigo, sculpted around 1500 with frescos perhaps by Lorenzo Lotto. The organ was built by Gaetano Callido in 1779.

Next to this church rises the former Dominican convent, a huge, mostly sixteenth-century building, which now serves as a seminary. Its chapter house dates from the late thirteenth century and has forty portraits of celebrated Dominicans, painted by Tommaso da Modena in 1352. Tommaso's signature appears to the right of the door. He was but twenty-six years old when he created this altogether delightful frieze. Each Dominican sits in his cell, writing or studying. Each is individual, alive, concentrating. Eighteen wear cardinals' hats; of seventeen other monks, two wear bishops' mitres. Papal tiaras identify Popes Innocent V and Benedict XI. Cardinal Ungo of Provenza wears glasses, the first time these useful articles had ever appeared in a portrait.

The province of Treviso is rightly dubbed 'joyful', the *marca gioiosa*, as the Italians call it. To explore this province take the road south-west out of Treviso from Porta Santi Quaranta towards Padua. At Quinto di Treviso (whose name refers to a Roman milestone) fresh fish from the Sile is caught and served in the local restaurants. Here stands the neo-classical Villa Ciardi. Next, at Santa Cristína al Tiverron, is a Gothic parish church, built in 1933, in which you discover an altarpiece of 1505 by Lorenzo Lotto depicting the dead Jesus. This part of the *marca* is scattered with watermills. And at Badoere, ten kilometres south-west, are the remains of a villa built by Angelo Badoer in 1756 and partly burned down in 1926.

North of here lies Istrana where, in a park laid out in the eighteenth century with statuary and fountains, stands Villa Tamagnino Lattes, which you can visit on weekday mornings (except on Mondays), and in the afternoon too at weekends. Giorgio Massari built the villa and its chapel in 1715 on behalf of his uncle, the Venetian noble Paolo Tamagnino, whose portrait hangs in the chapel. Today the villa, now the property of the commune of Treviso, houses the art collection of its last owner, Bruno Lattes. In its garden, with its wrought-iron gates, are statues of the twelve Caesars. Istrana also boasts a seventeenth-century parish church with an altar by Palma the Younger and frescos by Francesco Zugno.

Further north from Istrana, at Trevignano, is a classical church and a nineteenth-century villa with a huge portico. But my advice is to carry on west along the N53 towards the walled city of Castelfranco Véneto. On the way are two splendid villas. Near Vedelago, in the village of Sant'Andrea di Cavasagra, stands the late eighteenth-century Villa Corner della Regina, the work of Francesco Maria Preti. Today it is a hotel. And just beyond Vedelago, turn right for Fanzolo, where a double row of poplars leads to Palladio's superb Villa Emo, which he built in the first half of the 1560s. This villa is a majestic example of Palladio's skill at stretching out a long, horizontal complex. It ends in rustic dovecotes. Alessandro Vittoria sculpted the Emo coat of arms, supported by winged victories, for the tympanum of the loggia.

Around 1565 the mannerist Gian Battista Zelotti frescoed the interior, his figures apparently leaning out of the walls in *trompe-l'oeil* languor. You can visit Villa Emo at weekends in the afternoons, and this is also the venue of the Asolo music festival.

I have enjoyed staying at Castelfranco Véneto more than anywhere else in the Veneto. My lodgings are outside the walls, at the Locanda Speranza (or, in truth, in its splendid annex, to which I was led by the landlady, who rode her bicycle behind the trees, on the wrong side of the road, while I endeavoured to follow her in my car without hitting the trees on my side of the road).

One evening I remember thirty or so men – aged from twenty to around eighty, I judged – dining at the *locanda* seated at the three-sided table. They sang local songs and chattered much, emitting a hugely merry noise, which suddenly subsided when the food arrived. I was eating at the far end of the room with a couple who were staying overnight there, but they were as ignorant as I about this confraternity. The landlord, his wife and the waitress shot in and out of the kitchen, busy as beavers serving everyone, so I did not have the heart to waste their time asking questions (though now I wish I had done). Above the clamour, one ancient man rose and decided to drink my health. In return I clambered to my feet, said thank you, and for the rest of the evening my glass remained full, by courtesy of this confraternity.

That evening, as they served their guests, the landlord, his wife and the waitress ate their own evening meal in relays. If you ever stay here, I advise you to eat sparingly. The excellent *minestrone* alone is so thick and rich as virtually to slay the appetite. Each time I asked for a Grappa at the end of my meal the waitress would uncork its dusty bottle, sniff it and roll her eyes.

Castelfranco Véneto, founded in the year 1199, is surrounded by a tree-lined moat and twelfth-century walls made of thin red bricks. Today eighteenth-century statues lend glamour to the moat. The western side of the old city is encircled by modern arcades and shops. The old streets to the east have piazza bars and more shops. Through a handsome gateway set in the walls you walk on to the Piazza del Duomo with its grassy square and eighteenth-century statues by Orazio Marinali, depicting Romans and their ladies, at the end of it. The cathedral itself is massive, clean and classical, picked out in white and gold. Dedicated to Santissima Maria Assunta and San Liberale (Castelfranco's patron saint), it was built by Francesco Maria Preti (who lived from 1701 to 1774 and also built the theatre of Castelfranco, which stands in Via Garibaldi). Behind rises the Romanesque campanile.

Inside the cathedral are works by Giorgione, Paolo Veronese (who frescoed the sacristy), Bassano and Palma the Younger. The first of these artists is the most mysterious. Evidently born here (or nearby) in 1477 or 1478, he was baptized Giorgio, his surname was Barbarelli, but he was nicknamed Giorgione, apparently because his powerful frame matched his moral stature. He was also, as the gossip Giorgio Vasari noted, 'a most amorous man', a fact that eventually led to his undoing, for Giorgione could not stay away from his girlfriend even after she had contracted the plague. He caught it from her and died in 1510 in his early thirties (though some alleged that he had been assassinated).

Gabriele d'Annunzio allowed his considerable imagination free reign when he described his fellow-Venetan. 'No poet has had a comparable destiny on earth as he,' he wrote.

On no one painting can his name be inscribed with any certainty. Yet, in spite of this, the whole of Venetan art was enflamed by his revelation. From him Titian himself discovered the secret of infusing a luminous blood in the veins of those he painted.

For d'Annunzio, Giorgione's art was an 'epiphany of fire'. Like

Prometheus, Giorgione merited the description 'the bringer of fire'. Because of his warm, fiery colours, Italians coined the phrase *fuoco giorgionesco*.

Most of his paintings have disappeared. I have seen his 'Sleeping Venus' in Dresden and his portrait of Caterina Cornaro (whom we shall shortly meet at Altivale and Asolo) in the National Gallery in London, but this portrait was completed by Titian. The Ashmolean Museum in Oxford claims that a portrait of the Blessed Virgin Mary, reading a book, is also by Giorgione, but I doubt it. Outside Dresden, Castelfranco's cathedral is the sole place to find him, and here is only one painting, though it is a masterpiece. It serves as the altarpiece of a very plain chapel, with a knight's tomb and a recumbent statue on the floor. The knight is Matteo Constanza, a *condottiere* whose death in battle prompted his father to commission this altarpiece. Painted in 1504, it depicts the Madonna between St Francis and St Liberale. In the background are trees and the undulating landscape which he also beautifully deployed in Dresden's 'Sleeping Venus'. Next to the painting is a baroque statue, a Bernini-like Madonna in her Assumption, flanked by St Liberale and St John Nepomuk, the work of Canova's teacher Giuseppe Bernardi Tarretto (who lived from 1694 to 1773). At St Liberale's feet is a little town, said (no doubt wrongly) to have been sculpted by the infant Canova.

Next to the cathedral at Castelfranco is the so-called Giorgione's house, whose chiaroscuro façade may or may not have been frescoed by him. On the opposite side of the piazza is the city's elegant Prefettura. The arcaded street continues absolutely straight, past an ancient house frescoed with the Madonna and child, to a mighty double gateway, built of brick in the twelfth century, frescoed with the Carraresi coat of arms in the fourteenth, decorated with a winged lion and supporting a clock-tower. Outside is the handsome road that rings Castelfranco, lined with banks and bars. Walk on into Via Reccati. On the right rises the eighteenth-century church of San Giacomo Apostolo, built

145

by Giorgio Massari and housing works by Pietro della Vecchia, Pietro Damini and Egidio dall'Uglio.

A plaque on a little dusty house on the left proclaims that here Giuseppe Sarto lived between 1846 and 1850. The son of the village postman of nearby Riese, Giuseppe went to school at Castelfranco. He left to study at a Paduan seminary, was ordained in 1858 and then spent eight years as a country curate and nine as parish priest at Salzano. Subsequently Bishop of Mantua and Patriarch of Venice, he was elected Pope in 1903 (at the seventh ballot). Taking the name Pius X, he reigned until his death in 1914. Some say he performed miracles even in his lifetime, and in 1954 Pius X was declared a saint. I wish I found his deeply conservative theological views about the Bible congenial, but I do not.

Cross a bridge into Borgo Treviso to find first the eighteenth-century Palazzo Riccati degli Assoni Avogadro, with its imposing façade of 1908 and its leafy courtyard. Further on rises the sixteenth-century Palazzo Colonna Rainati, and then the pale pink, green and yellow Villa Revedin-Bolsaco. It was built in the nineteenth century by G. B. Meduna, though its park (which you can visit on Tuesday and Thursday afternoons, and on the afternoon of the first Sunday in the month), which has a lake and a Moorish greenhouse, was laid out in the eighteenth century, whence date its fifty or so statues by the Marinali family.

Eight kilometres north of Castelfranco is Riese, with the birthplace of Pope Pius X and, next door, a museum in his honour. North-east of Riese, at Altivole, find the Strada del Barco, alongside which is what remains of the Barco della Regina Cornaro, a Renaissance palace begun in 1491 on behalf of the former queen of Cyprus, Caterina Cornaro. Continue along the Strada del Barco, cross the road to Bassano del Grappa and you reach Coste, followed by Maser and one of Palladio's finest buildings.

Palladio built Villa Maser between 1560 and 1568 for two brothers, Mgr Eletto de Aquileia and Marcantonio de Barbaro.

He clearly revelled as much in the watered garden as in the villa, creating a fountain in the hillside opposite the house. 'This fountain forms a small lake, which serves as a fish-pond,' he wrote.

From this place the water runs into the kitchen; and after having watered the gardens that are on the right and left of the road, which leads gradually to the fabrick, it forms two fish-ponds, with their watering places upon the high-road; from whence it waters the kitchen garden, which is very large, and full of the most excellent fruits, and of different kinds of pulse.

The gardens are adorned with statues by Palladio's collaborator Alessandro Vittoria.

Villa Maser, which you can visit from mid-February to mid-November on Thursday, Saturday and Sunday afternoons, is unique among Palladio's villas at this time in lacking a portico. Its stuccoed pediment is Ionic, its interior decoration by Paolo Veronese revolutionary. 'De Barbaro was a great humanist – a translator of Vitruvius and himself interested in interior decoration,' noted Georgina Masson in her *Italian Villas and Palaces*.

It is believed that the choice of the style of decoration – the painted monochrome figures in niches and scenes with Roman ruins, especially in the cruciform central hall – may have been influenced by his ideas, though the general scheme was undoubtedly Veronese's.

Veronese introduced figures into *trompe-l'oeil* doors. He frescoed the garden room with mountain scenery, and painted the gods of Olympus on its ceiling. From the balcony his portraits of the Barbaro lords and ladies look down, accompanied by their pets, which include a brown and white dog, a parrot and a monkey. For this villa Palladio was able to build a chapel (the Tempietto), one of few of his works in the circular shape he so favoured for religious buildings. To see the inside you must attend Mass on Sunday morning.

You are now at the olive- and cypress-covered foothills of the Dolomites. West of Villa Maser, by way of Coste and Casella, look out for the signs pointing right to the enchanting hill town of Asolo. Halfway up is the sixteenth-century Villa Zen, built for Caterina Cornaro's nephew Pietro Zen, and opposite stands the church of San Gottardo, frescoed in the fourteenth century and now used for concerts.

The shades of two celebrated lovers, one Italian, the other British, haunt Asolo. The Italian is Pietro Bembo, who was born the son of a Venetian senator in 1470. A priest, domestic secretary to Pope Leo X, he fell in love with Morosina della Torre and she bore him three children. At Asolo he was a favourite at the court of Caterina Cornaro, who had relinquished her late husband's kingdom of Cyprus to the Venetian republic, which in return granted her a *castello* here and made her *signoria* of Asolo. She had made her entrance into Asolo on 11 October 1489, watched by 4,000 citizens, sheltered by a canopy carried by the noblest citizens of the town, 'complete' (as Vincent Cronin put it) 'with dwarf buffoon, hounds, apes and peacocks'. (The dwarf was a Moor named Zavir.)

As Cronin continues, 'Here, shut off from harsh reality by chestnut woods and a garden of bay-trees "so carefully cut that not a single leaf was out of place", Bembo used to discuss the nature of love.' His musings were published in 1505 in a book entitled *Gl' Asolani*. In the form of a dialogue, protagonists suggest that love is a kind of venom (as the words Venus and venery might suggest); that the bitterness provoked by love is well worth suffering for the joy it gives; and that a chaste kiss is the acme of loving, for it escapes the brutality of bodily lust. So this priest, who in real life had betrayed his vow of chastity, promulgated a notion of Platonic love that enthused the courtiers of Caterina Cornaro.

The second celebrated lover of Asolo is Robert Browning. Browning first reached Asolo at the age of twenty-six in 1838. After living in Italy for many years, he returned to London after his wife's death in 1861, seeing Asolo again only in 1882. Thenceforth he visited it for seven autumns. His *Asolando* was published in 1889, curiously on the day that he died at Ca' Rezzonico in Venice.

> How many a year, my Asolo,
> Since – one step just from sea to land –
> I found you, loved yet feared you so
> For natural objects seemed to stand
> Palpably fire-clothed

runs the prologue to *Asolando*. Browning took the title of this book of lyrics from Pietro Bembo's *Gl' Asolani*, and from the verb *asolare*, which Bembo defined as 'to disport in the open air, to amuse oneself at random'.

Asolo, Bembo wrote, 'is surrounded by a fairy garden of marvellous beauty', adding that neither San Gimignano, nor Siena, nor Volterra attracted him as much as this town, which from the day he first saw it 'dominated and enslaved me'. Set on its hill in a district of foothills, the Pedemontana, between the Rivers Brenta and Piave, Asolo is, as Gabriele d'Annunzio put it, a town of a hundred horizons. And to quote Browning again, seven weeks before his death he wrote to his brother-in-law George Moulton Barrett, 'This town fills me with admiration as it did fifty years ago. The immense enchantment of the landscape below is indescribable; I have never seen anything to equal it.'

Though the discovery of Neolithic pottery here indicates the age of the settlement, Asolo is a Renaissance town, with scarcely a medieval building, apart from its massive *rocca*, its surviving walls and the tower of Caterina's *castello*. An episcopal seat since 989, Asolo was subsequently ruled by the Ezzelini, the Scaligers, the Carraresi and the Trevignano, before coming under the suzerainty of Venice in the fourteenth century. With the coming of Queen Caterina Cornaro, the town reached its architectural apogee.

Shortly after her reign a villa was built on Via Canova which Browning was to buy. After his death it passed to his son Pen, whose marriage to an American heiress enabled him to indulge his passion for shooting, idling and languidly diverting himself. What he also did was found an embroidery school for the silk-workers of Asolo.

Happily, you can today stay where the Brownings once lived, for the Villa Galanti (as it was then called) is now the Hotel Villa Cipriani. This villa has an exquisite garden and breathtaking views. From the hotel you can see a fake villa on a hill, a stage-set that is just one room, and a real villa, the seventeenth-century Villa Contarini-Armeni. One faces west, the other south, and they are connected by a frescoed tunnel dug into the hillside, to provide both a summer and a winter residence.

Hotels of this calibre often serve an international cuisine, and this one is no exception; but my own recommendation is always to eat the dishes of the region – such as, in this case, *pasta e fagioli*, that splendidly thick soup with red borlotti beans and rings of pasta; *fegato alla veneziana*, that is calves' livers, sautéed with onions; and *vitello al prosecco*, veal sautéed in sparkling *prosecco* wine. A succulent pudding is *tirami sù*, a medley of chocolate, wine, coffee cake and fresh cream.

If you walk west from Villa Cipriani through arched houses down the cobbled Contradà Canova, you discover the house in which the great actress Eleonora Duse was born in 1859, its plaque singing her praises in words written by her lover d'Annunzio. Composed in 1925, a year after her death, it reads:

A ELEONORA DUSE
figlia ultimogenita di San Marco,
apparizione melodiosa
del patimento creatore
e della sovrana bontà.

(To Eleonora Duse
youngest daughter of San Marco,
sweet apparition

of the suffering Creator
and of the sovereign Goodness.)

Still further on, down the winding Via Santa Caterina, is the
Casa Longobarda, a little palace built around 1500, which once
belonged to Caterina Cornaro's architect Francesco Grazioli.
Admirers of Eleonora Duse will walk on to reach the Oasi
Santa Anna, where she is buried amid the cypresses. Following
her wish, her grave looks towards Monte Grappa.

Walking the other way from the Villa Cipriani down Via Canova
you reach the centre of Asolo, the triangular Piazza Gabriele
d'Annunzio. Beyond the arcaded, eighteenth-century Municipio
(which was built by Giorgio Massari as Palazzo Beltramini),
clamps hold together the medieval Torre dell'Orologio of Castel
Cornaro. Caterina's castle is today the Duse theatre. From its
terrace you look up to the ruined *rocca* and the cathedral
campanile. Another vista reveals the façade of Villa Scotti.

Via Regina Caterina runs downhill from the piazza to another
irregular piazza, named after Garibaldi, in which rises Asolo's
former cathedral of Santa Maria di Breda. Now the parish church,
it stands on the site of the Roman baths, was rebuilt in 1747 to the
design of Giorgio Massari and finished in the nineteenth century,
when the mosaics were added to its unfaced façade.

The *duomo* is even lower than the piazza, and you enter by
descending a flight of steps to discover an extraordinary treat:
a series of splendid paintings, all meticulously labelled, the best
found in the left-hand aisle. Here is Lorenzo Lotto's 'Assumption'
of 1506, which you can compare with that painted by Bassano
in the early 1560s. Lotto's Virgin Mary wears a cornflower blue
robe, and of his two saints Antony Abbot's beard juts out straight,
in the fashion of the time. Antony leans on the curious walking
stick that is his symbol. The other saint is Lodovico di Tolosa, and
both of them appear again in Bassano's 'Assumption'. Here I find
the Madonna a trifle wooden, ascending in a puff of smoke, but
the saints are exceedingly animated. As for the other paintings,

151

I do not believe that the portrait of St Francis of Assisi is really by Giovanni Bellini, but I like very much Sebastiano Bastiani's 1488 portrait of St Jerome, sitting on a throne, his pet lion at his feet.

At the age of sixteen, in a chapel in the same aisle, the future Pope Pius X received his tonsure. The cathedral's high altar is by Canova, with a couple of angels by Giuseppe Bernardi.

In the piazza is a fountain with a winged lion looking much fiercer than St Jerome's in the cathedral. Its waters arrive here by way of a Roman aqueduct. The Loggia del Capitano nearby was built in the fifteenth century and frescoed by A. Contarini in 1560. Today it is the civic museum, with mementoes of Eleonora Duse, d'Annunzio and Browning (including his spinet). Leave Piazza Garibaldi by Via Robert Browning, one side of which is arcaded. It curves past a lion fountain set in the wall in 1571, as far as the ancient walls and an equally ancient gate. At no. 153, sandwiched between two parts of a wine merchant's and an up-market grocery shop, is Casa Maffei, the house in which Browning rented a study, marked by a plaque inscribed:

IN QUESTA CASA
ABITÙ
ROBERTO BROWNING
SOMMO POETA INGLESE
VI SCRISSE
ASOLANDO
1889.

Now is the time for the energetic to return to Piazza Garibaldi, cross Piazza Angelo Brugnoli – which is overlooked by the splendid, three-storeyed Villa Scotti with its stepped garden – and climb by way of Via Dante past the villa to the *rocca*, where you are also rewarded with the seventeenth-century monastery church of Saints Peter and Paul.

Four years after he first reached Asolo, Robert Browning

published *Pippa Passes*. His Pippa is a silk-weaver of Asolo,
and on the first day of the year she is given a holiday. As she
wanders the streets, singing, her voice is heard in four houses,
whose tormented occupants are saved by its tones from evil.
Thus she sings as she passes:

> The year's at the spring,
> And day's at the morn;
> Morning's at seven;
> The hill-side's dew-pearled;
> The lark's on the wing;
> The snail's on the thorn;
> God's in his heaven;
> All's right with the world!

And so it often seems in Asolo.

It was not always so. The region was ravaged during the First
World War. 'When I open my bedroom shutters in the morning I
see Monte Grappa framed between them,' wrote Eleonora Duse.
'Then I place two bowls of flowers on the window-sill, to create
an altar. Contemplating it, I think of the dead of this last war,
and I want to cry.' War fortifications and trenches, bunkers,
shelters and tunnels dug by Austrians and Italians remain intact
on Monte Grappa. In ossuaries and little shrines rest the remains
of unknown soldiers. Local hiking associations have marked out
trails for those who wish to explore them. The Australian and
Italian dead sleep together in the chapel of the Madonnina
del Grappa. British soldiers lie in the cemetery at Giavera del
Montello, and the French in the cemetery at Pederobba. On
the Montello stands the monument to the Italian flying ace,
Francesco Baracca, precisely where his plane crashed fatally on
19 June 1918. It is inscribed with d'Annunzio's lines:

> *Di morte in morte.*
> *Di vittoria in vittoria.*
> *Così incomincia il suo inno senza lira.*
> *Così principia il salmo di questo Re!*

(From death to death.
From victory to victory.
So begins this hymn which knows not the sound of lyre.
So starts the psalm sung by this king!)

North-west of Asolo lies Possagno, the birthplace in 1757 of Antonio Canova. Beside the house in which he was born is the Gypsoteque, which serves as his museum, but his cold art is supremely represented here in the parish church. Designed by Canova, begun in 1819 and paid for out of his own pocket, this Pantheon-like building, approached by a broad flight of steps and fronted by a Doric portico, was finished in 1830, eight years after Canova's death. It enshrines his tomb (which he also designed) and a self-portrait bust, as well as his last work, a 'Deposition'.

South-east of Asolo is Montebelluna, the chief agricultural market of the province. Its former cathedral, Santa Maria in Colle, dates from the seventeenth century and contains an excellent two-manual organ built by G. Callido in 1805. The new cathedral is an amazing Gothic edifice of 1908.

Outside Montebelluna your route skirts the hills, through wine country, with vintners selling their produce by the roadside. Just beyond Venegazzu, beside a stream that runs off left from the main road, rises the classical Villa Spineda-Gasparini, with a detached pavilion. And at Nervesa della Battáglia (nearby which is an ossuary, containing the dust of some 10,000 soldiers from the First World War, as well as the ruined abbey of Sant'Eustachio), you join the main road running north from Treviso and cross the River Piave. Ahead rise the pink peaks of the Dolomites. Look out here for the impressive embankments, begun in the fourteenth century by Francesco da Carrara and finished in 1509 by Fra Giocondo.

The tower and fortifications of the fifteenth-century Castello di San Salvatore soon appear on the left, and at Susegana I recommend that you drive up the line of pollarded chestnuts that leads to its gate. This *castello* is private property, but from here you have a wonderful view of the plain. Susegana also has a parish church with remnants of Renaissance frescos and an altarpiece of the Madonna and child with four saints, painted by the young Giovanni Pordenone in 1515.

At Conegliano, seventeen kilometres north-east, you curve up the arcaded main street, in which rises the cathedral with its own Gothic arcade. Frescoed saints on pillars are dated 1471, one of them instantly recognizable as St Stephen about to die a martyr, from the stone which has hit his bleeding head and from his deacon's outfit. Conegliano was the birthplace in 1460 of Giovanni Battista Cima da Conegliano, and inside the cathedral is a retable of the Virgin in majesty, which he painted in 1493. Under the clock on its campanile appears the warning VULNERANT OMNES ULTIMA NECAT, signifying that everyone is likely to die.

The houses lining the arcaded streets of this town are sweet, nonchalantly differing in size, with decorated Gothic windows and sometimes with corner balconies. Opposite the theatre, built by A. Scala in 1866, in the Piazzetta 18 Luglio is a fifteenth-century well. The whole city is dominated by its medieval *castello*, now the local museum. Long ago Conegliano was protected by a gate and tower built by the Carraresi in 1384. Today they are toothlessly picturesque.

Other delights of Conegliano are the seventeenth-century Dominican church of San Martino, with a 1530 'Adoration of the Shepherds' by Francesco da Milano; the seventeenth-century church of San Rocco; and, beside the cathedral, the Scuola dei Battuti, which belonged to the Confraternity of the Flagellants and has a façade frescoed by Pozzoserrato in 1593.

Conegliano is proud both of its red and its white wines, and outside the city the vintners have signposted wine roads. The 'Strada del Vino Bianco' will take you west as far as San Pietro di Feletto, with its lovely Romanesque church, which was decorated with frescos between the twelfth and fifteenth centuries. Here you are not far from Follina, which boasts the finest Cistercian monastery in the Veneto. Founded in the twelfth century, its cloister of 1268 has twin columns and its fourteenth-century church has a triple Romanesque apse.

As you drive from Conegliano to Vittório Véneto, the scenery becomes breathtaking, with forest-clothed mountains rising steeply on either side and beds of rock outcropping in bare ribs. One might consider Vittório Véneto a curious jumble, until one remembers that this is in fact two former towns, industrialized Ceneda and ancient Serravalle, which were united only in 1866. The citizens still distinguish between them, as do their signposts.

Ceneda is the one you reach first. Its eighteenth-century cathedral, designed by Ottavio Scotti, has preserved a thirteenth-century campanile, paintings in the sacristy by Tiepolo and two fourteenth-century reredoses by Jacopo da Valenza. The great Sansovino built its former town hall in 1538. The fourteenth-century church of Sant'Andrea di Bigonzo has a little portico. At Serravalle you suddenly enter another world, a city of streets watered by the River Meschio and narrow, arcaded alleyways. The loveliest of these is Via Martiri della Libertà, which is flanked by Gothic and Renaissance houses and opens into Piazza Marc'Antonio Flaminio. Among the old palaces of this piazza is the former town hall, the Gothic Loggia Serravallese of 1462, which is carried on Roman arches, its façade covered in escutcheons.

At the end of this piazza is Vittório Véneto's second *duomo*, this one also built in the eighteenth century. Beside the apse rises its detached, bare campanile, dating from the fourteenth and sixteenth centuries. Inside, the décor of the 1770s is by A. Schiava da Tolmezzo. G. B. Canaletto frescoed the cathedral's ceiling with a *trompe-l'oeil* view of heaven. Its high altar bears a 1547 painting by Titian of the Madonna and child, with Saints Andrew and Peter. Peter wears a splendid red cloak and is handing his keys to the Virgin. Andrew's huge cross reaches to heaven. In the distance Titian has added the New Testament scene of the miraculous draught of fishes. This is an imposing painting, but

I think I prefer Francesco da Milano's 'Annunciation' on the left, its archangel animated, Mary modest. On the right he has painted St Andrew and St Peter, St Catherine with her wheel and St Lucy with her eyes on a plate.

Follow Via Roma from the Loggia Serravallese, and then Via Mazzini, to find the fourteenth-century church of San Giovanni Battista, with its Renaissance portal underneath a rose window. The Romanesque campanile is satisfyingly simply, the cloister Renaissance. Inside are paintings by Jacopo da Valenza and Francesco da Milano, while the fifteenth-century frescos include the scene of St Nicholas handing a poor girl her dowry through a window and a hideous martyrdom.

On 21 and 22 August pilgrims reach Vittório Véneto to climb 349 metres to the sanctuary of St Augusta, which was built in the sixteenth century. You reach it from the monumental steps that lead up to a statue of Augusta, just beyond the cathedral. From here a zigzag route runs beside votive chapels and the fragmentary walls of the city (built around 1200), ending in an extremely steep flight of steps. The walk took me some forty minutes. The barrel-vaulted sanctuary has been well restored. And here is a holy well. Thank heavens there is also a small *trattoria*.

Belluno and the Dolomites

Autumn is a romantic season in the Veneto and, except for those who want to swim, November is a fine time to visit the region – sometimes cold, sometimes surprisingly warm, and at times a mist hovers over the rivers and in the valleys.

To cross the pass from Vittório Véneto into the province of Belluno, on one of those November days when the sun shines, is enthralling, especially if you eschew the motorway (though on its stilts it is in places almost as spectacular as the scenery). The secondary road climbs and perilously winds. Savage crags of the Dolomites appear ahead. As the road descends into the province of Belluno, these crags, and the brown and green vegetation of the hillside, are reflected in a huge lake.

The setting of Belluno is equally stunning, on a plateau where the Rivers Piave and Ardo meet. The 2,250-metre-high Cavallo massif shelters the city to the east, while to the north rise the 2,133-metre-high Monte Serva and the 2,563-metre-high Monte Schiara. To the west rise Monte Pizzocco and Monte Vedana, both of them topping 2,000 metres. In consequence Belluno has prospered above all, in the last hundred years, as a winter sports centre, serving both alpinists and experienced skiers.

The sight of its lovely monuments is a reminder that Belluno has also prospered in past centuries. Archaeologists have unearthed finds dating back to the fifth century BC. Again, as we have so often seen in the Veneto, a chequerboard pattern of streets bespeaks the influence of the Romans. And from the Middle Ages Belluno has preserved its twelfth-century Porta Ruga, the thirteenth-century Torre Civica, and the thirteenth-century Porta Doiona, though this was rebuilt in 1553.

Begin a visit at the Piazza del Duomo, where on Saturdays you will find a little flower market. The cathedral of Santa Maria Assunta is but one of the splendid buildings that enhance this piazza. On the north side of the piazza the Torre Civica remains from the former palace of the episcopal-counts of Belluno. Beside it stands the Renaissance Palazzo dei Rettori, built in 1491 for the Venetian governors of the city, the Podestàs. Arcaded, with twin windows, it clearly displays the influence of contemporary Venetian architecture, in spite of the multitude of entertaining, if incongruous, baroque busts and coats of arms covering its façade.

The town hall, rising on the west side of the piazza, adds another piquantly incongruous note. Incorporating the former Palazzo della Caminada, this is a pink and white Gothic creation of 1838 by the architect Giuseppe Segusini. To the west stands the Palazzo dei Giurati, now the city museum and art gallery. To my mind its finest paintings are those of the mannerist Palma the Younger, who lived from 1548 to 1628. Other works include paintings by Sebastiano Ricci, who was born at Belluno in 1659, and by Bartolomeo Montagna.

As for the cathedral itself, Tullio Lombardo, best known for the church of San Salvatore in Venice, designed it in the early sixteenth century. But what first strikes the eye is not his façade – which has never been finished – but the swaggering baroque campanile, added by Filippo Juvara in 1743 and rising for sixty-six metres. A bronze Archangel Michael on top of the campanile is about to blow his trumpet to signal the Last Judgement. And, on the north side of the building, former bishops of Belluno have affixed their coats of arms. On another wall is a fifteenth-century, sadly damaged crucifixion.

Inside, Tullio Lombardo's sensitivities reassert themselves. He built the cathedral out of Dolomite stone, dividing it into three naves. For the first altar on the left he sculpted a couple of exquisite, small statues, depicting St Lucianus and St Jonathan. Other artists add to the pleasures of visiting this cathedral, particularly Palma the Younger (who painted an 'Entombment' and a 'Martyrdom of St Laurence' for the fourth altar on the right), but also Jacopo Bassano, Andrea Schiavone and Cesare Vecellio. The last, who was born at Pieve di Cadore in 1521, has left us a complex painting of the martyrdom of St Sebastian. Sebastian looks up to heaven, from where the Virgin Mary and her infant son, flanked by angels, look down in compassion. Looking up too is St Fabian, in his papal tiara. He is recognizable by the dove flapping over his head, for when he was elected Pope in the year 236, the assembled bishops were informed that Fabian was God's choice by the Holy Spirit appearing in this form and settling on his head. A third figure in this painting is not looking up to heaven. This is Podestà, who presumably commissioned the painting.

The Madonna and child appear in another sixteenth-century painting in this cathedral, this one in the baptistry and by an unknown artist. Again, a small kneeling lady in this picture must be the donor. A triple tier of seventeenth-century stalls is to be seen in the apse, and there are lovely eighteenth-century marble altars.

Mary and her divine son are also depicted in the double-aisled crypt. An unknown but extremely talented sculptor carved them in the fourteenth century. They are flanked by saints, including Peter and Paul, and by Mary's mother, while on either side of her throne kneel the donors. A finely carved fourteenth-century sarcophagus serves as an altar in this crypt. Its reredos is superb, a fourteenth-century polyptych by Simon da Cusighe depicting scenes from the life of St Martin of Tours. In the central panel Martin slices his cloak in half, to give one part to a naked beggar. The saint looks down kindly, his magnificent horse haughtily, as if to ask why on earth this beggar is troubling his master.

Walk left of the elaborate city museum to reach the Piazza del Mercato, whose fruit and vegetable market is cooled by a fountain of 1410 on which stands a sculpted bishop. Here rises Belluno's Monte-del-Pietà of 1510. From Piazza del Mercato, Via Mezzaterra runs south, a confection of Renaissance palaces, some of them frescoed. Turn left into the narrow, buttressed Vicolo San Pietro to find the church of San Pietro, once again filled with paintings by artists of the calibre of Andrea Schiavone. Pigeons perch on the church façade.

Belluno is much enhanced by its arcaded streets and piazzas, which include Via Roma and Piazza San Stefano into which it leads. Once a sarcophagus stood in this piazza, and it ought still to be here. It was created in the third century AD for a Roman named Caius Flavius Ostilius and his wife Domitia. This Roman evidently adored the setting of ancient Belluno and deliberately chose this spot for his tomb, for its Greek inscription proclaims, 'Flavius, continue to enjoy what you have always loved of these mountains.' The sarcophagus has been moved to the city museum. Whether or not Flavius does still enjoy the mountains, nearby Via Flavio Ostilio is a spot in which to pause and relish the superb landscape surrounding the city.

San Stefano itself is Gothic, built in 1468, though the building incorporates a fourteenth-century portal. Its tall Gothic aisles, rising on pink and white columns of different dimensions, shelter works by Bassano and Vecellio (who painted the 'Annunciation' in the nave), a carving of Jesus crucified by Andrea Brustolon and the golden Madonna della Salute by A. di Foro. Here is a baroque statue of St Barbara and frescos of St Stephen and St Paul by a pupil of Mantegna. Noble Belluno families lie buried in the aisles.

The campanile dates from 1780. And a treat is a Gothic doorway, brought here in 1892. Very lovely it is, depicting the Blessed Virgin gathering the faithful, along with God the Father and the four patron saints of Belluno. The building beside San Stefano has a sandstone façade and was once a Servite monastery, but the Servite fathers were expelled from their lovely cloister in 1806.

Early eighteenth-century masters who built splendid villas included the Paduan Alessandro Tremignon. In 1711 he designed the imposing Villa Vescovile in the Belluno suburb of Belvedere for the city's bishop, Giovanni Francesco Bembo. It is open to visitors most days, if you telephone in advance (0437-25262).

Winter sports fanatics leave Belluno for the forested regions that surround the town of Agordo, twenty-nine kilometres north-west. Though the Dolomites are sixty million years old, they were named only 200 years ago, and after a Frenchman, not an Italian. Dieudonne Sylvain Guy Tancrède de Gratet de Dolomieu is almost as renowned for his love affairs as for his geological discoveries. He pioneered the study of these superb mountains, which are made of calcium and magnesium. Glaciers, earthquakes and torrents have chiselled them; humans settled here some 150,000 years ago, leaving behind the remains of lake villages.

Near Agordo, Monte Civetta rises to 3,220 metres and Monte Talavena to 2,542 metres. The Agordino district has 270 kilometres of ski-slopes, and another 160 kilometres prepared for cross-country skiing. Refuge huts sit on itineraries that encompass the Alte Vie (which the authorities recommend only for adventurous hikers). Here grow bilberries and dwarf pines. Deer and marmots roam the snow-covered valleys and hills. Some 2 million visitors stay annually in the Agordino alone, which has 150 hotels and six camp sites, not to speak of two ice stadia, six skating rinks, forty-two ski-lifts and six cableways.

Admirers of Titian will make their way north-east from Belluno, alongside the River Piave until they reach Pieve di Cadore, where the artist (whose proper name was Tiziano Vecellio) was born around 1485. His home is now a museum, and the frescos on the house next door are claimed to be by the youthful artist himself. A more reliable attribution is that of a painting of the Madonna and child in the parish church. Mary and Jesus are accompanied by St Andrew and the artist's own patron saint (St Tiziano), while Titian himself appears portrayed as the donor of the painting.

The charms of Pieve di Cadore were enhanced in 1949 when the River Piave was dammed to create an artificial lake, the Pieve. Monte Cristallo, the Marmarole and the Tre Cime di Lavoredo are mountain peaks in this region, while the lower ground is threaded by the River Piave. Small wonder that over 1 million visitors arrive here annually.

Further north-east Sappada, on the very edge of the Veneto, displays Tyrolean architecture. Here, as well as Italian, the citizens speak their own ancient German language. Even the bars are called *Stuben*. Carnival is celebrated German-fashion, with people wandering the streets in fancy dress. The annual summer pilgrimage from Sappada is not to any Venetan shrine but to Santa Maria di Luggau in Austria.

Just before you reach Sappada, at San Pietro di Cadore, stands the northernmost villa of the Veneto. Baldassare Longhena built the massive Villa Poli de Pol in 1665, and Girolamo Pellegrini frescoed its rooms in 1682. By telephoning in advance (0435-460014) you can visit the villa from Monday to Saturday between 08.00 and 13.00 and on Tuesday and Wednesday afternoons.

Summertime at Sappada encourages horse-riding. Winter, which lasts from December to April, is when the fifty kilometres of ski-slopes come into their own. The ski-instructors welcome the New Year with a torchlight procession on 31 December.

From Pieve di Cadore a scenic 30-kilometre drive along the valley of the Bóite reaches Cortina d'Ampezzo, which stands 1,210 metres above sea-level and is the best-known sports resort of the Dolomites. On the way, in the river valley, are sanctuaries dedicated to the Madonna della Difesa, so called because the

163

Blessed Virgin here defends the inhabitants from landslides and floods. In 1510, at San Vito di Cadore, her image was equally useful when the Germans were ravaging the region. Their troops sacrilegiously entered her sanctuary, at which the image suddenly flew from its pedestal, struck a few of them and so terrified the rest that they slew themselves.

At Cortina d'Ampezzo cable-cars rise perilously to various peaks: the 1,539-metre-high Belvedere di Pocol to the south-west; to the south-east the 2,343-metre-high Tondi di Faloria (where, in a square tower, lie the remains of 7,725 soldiers killed in the First World War); and to Le Tofane, rising 3,243 metres to the west and offering a panorama that stretches to the Venetian lagoon itself. In spite of this view of the lagoon, it is hard to believe that Cortina d'Ampezzo is but a two-hour drive from La Serenissima.

The eighteenth-century parish church at Cortina d'Ampezzo invites you to enjoy a similar panoramic view from its 76-metre-high campanile (which was built in 1863). The town also boasts an Olympic ice stadium, a geological museum and, finally, a monument to the geologist Dolomieu. The environs of Cortina d'Ampezzo include 160 kilometres of ski-pistes, some of them perilous. More than seventy kilometres of ski-slopes cater for the less skilled, as do professional schools teaching cross-country and downhill skiing. In this region, as well as the Olympic ice stadium, there is an Olympic ski-jump and an artificially refrigerated Olympic bob-sleigh piste.

Another spectacular route from Belluno, this time running south-west along the left bank of the Piave, leads to another gem of the province, Feltre. All along the route, on the right, rise crags looking like rotting teeth. On the way you pass through Mel, with its eighth-century BC necropolis. The streets of Mel, and the Piazza Umberto I, are shaded by Renaissance and baroque houses. In the attractively decayed Piazza Papa Luciani the eighteenth-century church has paintings by Vecellio and Schiavone. Schiavone also painted an altarpiece in the Chiesa del Addolorata, whose font dates from 1481.

Before crossing the River Piave before you get to Feltre, you reach Lentiai, where the Renaissance parish church of Santa Maria Assunta was built in the sixteenth century. Vecellio frescoed its walls and created the painting on the left of the choir, and Palma the Younger also contributed his own works to the church.

Feltre is almost as splendidly sited as Belluno. Ancient gates protect each entrance to the city's medieval main street, the Via Mezzaterra, some of whose Renaissance houses are gaily painted. The finest ensemble of the city is undoubtedly its Piazza Vittorio Emanuele. Rising up the hillside, surrounded by arcaded Renaissance homes and some splendid Gothic ones, it centres on a column bearing the lion of St Mark and statues of Vittorino da Feltre and Panfilo Castaldi. Vittorino was a teacher, born here in 1378. (He died at Mantua in 1446.) Panfilo (described on his statue as a man of generous spirit) was a typographer, born here in 1398 and depicted setting printer's type.

Above this piazza, weather-worn steps lead to an equally weather-worn medieval castle. From the castle, the narrow Salito Bernardino Guslini (which takes its name from a jurist who lived from 1534 to 1580) winds down to Via Lorenzo Luzzo – named after Feltre's most celebrated son, the fifteenth-century artist who called himself Morto da Feltre – also almost entirely flanked by Renaissance houses. The double-balconied house at no. 23 is the Palazzo Villabruna, today the city museum, whose gallery displays not only works by Morto da Feltre but also a portrait by Gentile Bellini and some eighteenth-century works by Bellotto. Another painting by Morto da Feltre (and one reckoned as his masterpiece), a picture of Jesus appearing after his resurrection, hangs in the church of Ognissanti in Via Belluno. This church also has a painting by Tintoretto of the Virgin Mary between St Nicholas of Bari and St Victor. The end of the street is closed by the Porta Oria.

Below the grassy Piazza Vittorio Emanuele a fountain of 1520, by Tullio Lombardo, gushes in the piazza of the church of San Rocco, built in 1599 and boasting a classical façade.

Another attractive façade fronts the Venetian Gothic Palazzo Guarnini, which was built in 1850. The cathedral is reached by a delightfully circuitous route from here, down the steps beside the Palladian Municipio (on which a plaque proudly announces that Goldoni worked here in 1729 and 1730). Salita Vittore dal Pozzo (named after a soldier who died in 1530) twists and burrows under buildings, its marble and cobbled steps flanked by quiet arcades.

The *duomo* lies outside the city wall (through which the Salita burrows). It has a Renaissance doorway, beside which a monument of 1473 depicts a knight lying most uncomfortably. Tullio Lombardo designed a tomb for the choir of Feltre's cathedral. Though its polygonal apse is fifteenth-century Gothic and most of the rest of the cathedral was rebuilt in the following century, its crypt dates from the ninth century, supported by simple pillars, and its campanile was raised in 1392. The neighbouring baptistry, though built in the fifteenth century, has a fine classical façade.

Feltre has its legends and its festivals. Here, as at San Vito di Cadore, the Blessed Virgin is said to have repulsed the imperial troops in 1510. On 11 July the citizens barricaded themselves inside the cathedral, kneeling before her image and beseeching her help. The enemy troops found themselves unable to smash down the doors. They set fire to the building, but the flames did no damage. In vain they fired grenades against it. Finally, realizing that they were up against divine intervention, they retired in dismay.

This city united with Venice in 1404, and in July it celebrates the fact with a colourful *palio*. Men, women and children dress in fifteenth-century costume, parading up Via Mezzaterra as far as Piazza Vittorio Emanuele, where they indulge in an archery contest, followed by a magnificent display of flag-waving.

At Santi Vittore e Corona, not four kilometres south-east of Feltre, stands a curiosity: a Romanesque-Byzantine church, begun in 1096 and frescoed in the thirteenth, fourteenth and fifteenth centuries. Beside it is a monastery built in 1495 and rising high up on the left of the SS348. This is as picturesque a road as any in the province, spectacularly sited amid the mountains. The River Piave cuts through them, with tree-covered cliffs climbing high on either side until you reach Fener, on the border of the province.

And here my book ends, with a reminder of those words on the plaque on Ca' Rezzonico in Venice, where Robert Browning died on 12 December 1889. They strike chords in the heart of any lover of the Veneto. The plaque quotes Browning's own assertion: 'Open my heart and you will see graved inside of it "Italy".'

Bibliography

Joseph Addison, *Remarks on Several Parts of Italy etc. in the Years 1701, 1702, 1703,* J. &. R. Tonson, 1767.

Mario De Biasi and Diego Valeri, *Lago di Garda,* Editrice dell'Automobile, Rome, 1959.

Bruce Boucher, *The Sculpture of Jacopo Sansovino,* Yale University Press, 1992.

Vincent Cronin, *The Flowering of the Renaissance,* Collins, 1969.

Antonio Canova, *Ville del Polesine,* Instituto Padano di Arti Grafiche, Rovigo, 1986.

John Evelyn, *The Diary of John Evelyn, Esq.,* edited by William Bray, Fred Warne and Co., 1891.

John McAndrew, *Venetian Architecture of the Early Renaissance,* The MIT Press, Cambridge, Massachusetts, 1980.

Anna B. MacMaham, *With Byron in Italy,* T. Fisher Unwin, 1907.

Georgina Masson, *Italian Villas and Palaces,* Thames and Hudson, 1959.

Giovanni Nepi (introduction), *Treasures of Venetian Painting* (devoted to the Galleria dell'Accademia, Venice), Thames and Hudson, 1991.

Andrea Palladio, *The Four Books of Architecture*, Dover Publications Inc., New York, 1965.

Freya Stark, 'An English Defence of Asolo', in *Country Life*, 7 October 1971.

Index